God's Opinion on Today's

hottest

SEX

topics

JOE CAMENETI

God's Opinion on Today's

hottest
SEX
topics

HONOR ✠ NET
THE HONOR NETWORK

TULSA OKLAHOMA

God's Opinion on Today's Hottest Sex Topics

ISBN 10: 0-9788726-5-7
ISBN 13: 978-0-9788726-5-6

Pastor Joe Cameneti
2577 Schenley Avenue NE
Warren, OH 44483
Web site: www.pastorjoe.com

Produced by HonorNet

Dedication

This book is dedicated to my children and to their generation. May these young Christian men and women rise above the culture of their day and live holy lives that please God, their heavenly father. May they also model this lifestyle to their world as they share the message of Christ with them! I'm expecting their generation to raise the standard and please God concerning the area of sexual activity!

Contents

WHEN IT COMES TO SEX, "This ain't your father's generation!" This current generation uses sex to sell just about anything from gum to tires! They are very comfortable walking into a clothing store that has, at best, posters of half dressed men and women marketing clothes that they aren't wearing! We can flip on the television and hear one sexual comment after another, see everything hanging out and watch a very sensual sex scene, with some token clothes on, or see girls kissing and falling in love with each other—and all of this on free television—without ever having to turn to premium channels. Should we choose to, we can watch pure pornography anytime of the day on a pay channel or, of course, on the Internet for free and pay. Sex truly is being displayed everywhere and society is telling us it's okay; it's normal to practice free sex.

This book isn't a crusade to try and shove my personal values down anyone's throat.

I really don't like that approach for many reasons. At one time in my life, before I met Jesus as my personal Savior, I was one of the people who was sex-crazed and pornography-addicted. At that time no one could push their moral values on me, because I wouldn't listen. What captured my attention was the man who shared Christ with me. He didn't condemn me, and he could have. He simply loved me and told me about Jesus.

My heart in writing this book is to instruct those who confess to be Christians, those who believe the Bible is God speaking to mankind. If you're reading this book as a non-confessing Christian, I trust you understand that whether or not you practice free sex, you can't go to heaven unless you trust in Christ as your Savior. According to the Bible, He truly is the only way God's provided for all mankind to enter the pearly gates (John 14:6, Romans 6:23, Acts 4:12). I'd love for you to hear my story concerning how I accepted Christ as my personal Savior. You can view my personal story on my Web site, "pastorjoe.com." Even if you're not a Christian, this book will open your eyes to the heart and motive of God in the area of sexual activity. I believe that will be a good thing for you and it will add a perspective that can save you much heartache in the future or at least help you to understand the Christian mindset.

I've observed that many Christians—especially the younger generation—don't understand what God has to say about today's hottest sex topics. Their moral beliefs have been formed by the distorted sexual bombardment they've been subject to from birth. That's my number-one reason for writing this book, to help all Christians understand the personal choices God wants us to make in these areas. We'll talk about such things as: Can sex be enjoyed and really, really fun for a Christian? Can you have sex when you're not married? Is sexual fantasizing and foreplay okay to do? Can we sleep around or enjoy pornography when we're married? Is sex with someone of the same sex okay? Is gay marriage okay? Can a person be born gay? What does God think about abortion? And, oh, the next two topics are so important in my opinion: How does God want Christians to treat those who sin sexually or commit any type of sin and how can a person overcome sexual sin?

I can boldly say that God doesn't want us looking down on people who aren't following the Bible. He does want us to have a heart that will reach out to them, sharing Christ in love, and remembering that we are what we are only by the grace of God. As a pastor, I am well aware of the need for Christians to be educated in this area, and I'm excited that this book will do just that! Get ready to go on a journey and discover God's opinion on today's hottest sex topics!

God's Opinion?

YOU MAY HAVE LOOKED at the title of this book— *God's Opinion on Today's Hottest Sex Topics*—and wondered, *How can Pastor Joe have the nerve to think that he knows God's opinion?* Well, it is true that Jesus didn't sit with me over a double espresso and fill me in on His opinion of the hottest sex topics of our day. Nor did He take me up to heaven, show me around, and talk to me about His opinion. I'd love to make up a story and tell you that I did go to heaven—so I could get you to send me a special offering or sign your house over to me, but I didn't! Yet I do have some knowledge on the topic because God gave us the Bible.

He really did inspire men to write the Bible, which we Christians also call, the Word. Let's first find out what the Bible has to say about itself.

The Bible is God speaking to mankind.

> *But as for you, continue in what you have learned and have become convinced of, because you know those from whom you learned it, and how from infancy you have known the holy Scriptures, which are able to make you wise for salvation through faith in Christ Jesus. **All Scripture is God-breathed** and is useful for teaching, rebuking, correcting and training in righteousness, so that the man of God may be thoroughly equipped for every good work.*
> —2 Timothy 3:14-17 (emphasis mine)

Timothy grew up reading the Bible, God's Word, and it led him to Christ. In the passage just referenced, Paul commended Timothy and encouraged him to continue reading and doing what the Bible says. Timothy was pastoring a church at the time. Notice Paul's words: "All Scripture is God-breathed." This means that the words in the Bible came out of God's mouth—He is speaking to mankind through the pages of the Bible.

We know that certain men were chosen to write the Bible, but the important thing to remember is that *God inspired them*. The Holy Spirit gave them divine inspiration, and they wrote down what He said. Their writings include God's opinion and His plan concerning everything that has to do with you and all of mankind. In this book, we're looking at specific Scriptures that tell us what God says about sex. In the verses just referenced, He mentions four uses for the Scriptures—two of which are teaching and training in righteousness. That is the purpose of this book: to teach and train Christian people—especially young people—in God's way concerning sex.

We live in a society today that has some very, very hot issues when it comes to sex. Gay marriage is probably one of the hottest issues right now, and people are constantly debating it. Men are marrying men, and women are marrying women.

> God created us—man and woman—as sexual beings, and His opinion is the one that should count for us Christians.

I'm sure most of these people are awesome people, with good hearts and exceptional talents! Yet there is a great deal of controversy about marriage between the same sex, and most everyone has an opinion. But the big question is, "What does God have to say about it?" God created us—man and woman—as sexual beings, and His opinion is the one that should count for us Christians.

If you're a Christian I don't have to convince you that the Bible is God speaking to mankind. I remember how I was before I trusted in Christ and the difference that took place the moment I accepted Him as my personal Savior. I remember the time, before Christ was my Savior, when I didn't feel bad when I sinned. I could do anything, from sexual things to stealing, and never feel remorse. I did not feel guilty about my lifestyle. After I accepted Christ, before I knew any scriptures, I immediately knew I should stop smoking weed, watching pornography, stealing, lying, cheating, and the list goes on.

I didn't know it at the time, but the Bible says when we accept Christ as our Lord and Savior that God, the Holy Spirit, comes to live inside of us and He convicts us of our sin. Did He ever convict me of sin! The day after I accepted Christ, I remember finding my brother Tony in the office reading one of the many pornography books we had there. Remember, I'd read all those same magazines just the day before, but now I couldn't stand them—not because any Christians or preachers told me to stop, but because I'd simply prayed and accepted Christ as my Savior.

When I saw Tony reading a girly magazine, I grabbed it along with the entire stack of books, threw them in the garbage, and said, "This is sin, Tony, and it will send you to hell! I accepted Jesus as my personal

Savior last night, and you need to get saved yourself!" He was really mad at me and nearly punched me as he stormed out of the office! I must admit my approach was terrible and I deserved a punch! From that time on, not only did I know what was and was not sin, but I also knew that I knew that the Bible was God speaking to mankind! Yet, although I knew what sin was, I still had to grow spiritually and learn what the Bible had to say about these things and how to overcome them.

I'm convinced that the Bible is truth, and I trust God will convince you if you're not already convinced. All of us also realize that the truth in the Bible can be twisted. We've all heard a crazy preacher take one verse and make it say what they want! Those types of people scare me, and I'm sure they scare you! Consider these words to Timothy from Paul:

> *Be diligent to present yourself approved to God, a worker who does not need to be ashamed, **rightly dividing <u>the word of truth</u>**.*
> —2 Timothy 2:15 NKJV (emphasis mine)

The "word of truth" is the Bible and it can be rightly divided. God used Paul to tell Timothy to make sure that he was rightly dividing it. If the Bible must be rightly divided or interpreted correctly, then it can very easily be wrongly divided! Interpreting Scripture is extremely serious business, and ministers have an awesome responsibility to make sure their interpretations come from God. I can assure you that this is my goal. I want to make sure that everyone who reads this book clearly understands God's position on sexual behavior. I also realize that I'm not perfect and only Jesus was and is! So you also have the responsibility of reading the Bible and finding out the truth for yourself. You should check what I say and make sure it's in the Bible and that I'm properly interpreting it.

You also have the responsibility of reading the Bible and finding out the truth for yourself.

The New Testament book of Acts is a historical record of the early church and also covers the spiritual work of two of the greatest apostles—Peter and Paul. Peter was centrally involved in the church's beginning in Jerusalem, and Paul was the important missionary who went out to nearby countries to tell others about Christ. Look at what Paul had to say about a community that accepted his message about Christ—a community that took personal responsibility to search and examine the Scriptures, for which they had great reverence, to find out if what Paul was saying was really in the Bible.

> *And the people of Berea were more open-minded than those in Thessalonica, and they listened eagerly to Paul's message. **They searched the Scriptures day after day to check up on Paul and Silas**, to see if they were really teaching the truth.*
>
> —Acts 17:11 NLT (emphasis mine)

It's easy to see that though Paul and Silas had come to this city to preach the gospel to the local people, those folks didn't just blindly accept what they said as truth until they had checked into the Scriptures for themselves. I encourage you to do the same. I pray and study and do my best to rightly divide the Word of God, but you need to check out the Bible for yourself and make sure that I'm teaching the truth.

Why is it so important to know God's opinion about sex or any other subject? It is because we must know the truth in order to please God, and truth can only be found in the Bible. If we don't know what God thinks—and we don't unless we know what the Bible says—then what's going to happen in our lives and in our communities? The following verse illustrates what will take place in the lives and communities of those that don't understand what the Bible is saying about sex or other moral issues.

*Where there is no revelation, **the people cast off restraint**; but blessed is he who keeps the law.*
—Proverbs 29:18 NIV (emphasis mine)

*When people do not accept divine guidance, **they run wild**. But whoever obeys the law is happy.*
—Proverbs 29:18 NLT (emphasis mine)

The latter part of this verse provides important information about how to be happy and blessed: We do it by keeping the law. The law, in this context—interpreted for the Christian church—refers to God's rules and regulations for how we should live our lives as individuals and in our Christian communities. God's law is found in the Bible, so when we obey the Bible, God's word to mankind, we not only find truth but also happiness and blessings.

The first part of this verse tells us what happens when a person doesn't know what the Bible says and/ or doesn't obey what the Bible instructs them to do. We run wild! We have infomercials of "Girls Gone Wild" today, because we live in a society that doesn't believe the Bible is God speaking to mankind. Where there's no revelation of the Bible, people cast off restraint— anything goes. I know in my own life the Bible is a restraint that keeps me from doing certain things. Knowing God's opinion changes the way we live and the choices we make! Again, on top of that, if we find out what God says to do and do it, the Bible says we will be happy and blessed. Some amazing statistics, that we'll look at in this book, prove that people who obey the Bible are actually the happiest people on earth, and that includes sexual happiness.[1] But "when people do not accept divine guidance, they truly "run wild." That wild lifestyle brings much heartache to them and to society!

As I said earlier, I am not an activist, and I'm not coming against any individual or group of people. I'm not trying to make non-Christians live according to Bible standards. I'm writing this for the majority of people in the United States of America who declare themselves to be Christians, but don't really know what the Bible has to say about sexual issues. I love this nation, but as I look around, I see many people who are running around performing some very wild and crazy acts. I understand that

> These senseless killing sprees were not happening just a generation ago, but now all kinds of wild and bizarre things are taking place.

people, especially young people who are just learning the Bible, are going to make mistakes just as we did when we were young, but take a good look at what's happening in our nation. High school and college-age kids are taking weapons to school and killing fellow students and faculty. I'm sure you would agree that this is wild behavior that should not be happening. In fact, these senseless killing sprees were not happening just a generation ago, but now all kinds of wild and bizarre things are taking place, and not only among the youth. Even adults are running wild and doing crazy things.

Many of our young people today have grown up in a society where good morals have fallen by the wayside. Without anyone to teach them biblical morals, many are caught up in all kinds of sins, including sexual sins that not only harm them but also others. I think there is a connection to Judeo-Christian values not being taught to this younger generation and what's going on in society. The harness is off and people are running crazy! Allow me to paint a picture of the moral climate of our nation concerning the topic of sex.

I can do so by reviewing facts from a November 2003 survey conducted by one of the leading market research firms that specializes in the study of religious beliefs and the behavior of Americans, The Barna Group, based in Ventura, California. The study reveals some interesting statistics about the hottest sex topics of our day. In this survey, different age groups were asked this question about several sex topics: "Do you feel these things are morally acceptable?" The statistics—including a cross section of society of all ages, a group of young people 18-21 years old, and another group of people 58 years old and older—may surprise you. These statistics represent the responses of the current generation—the first generation to grow up with point-and-click pornography on the Internet. Almost 90 percent of them have viewed porn online, and most of them did it while doing homework. They also see almost 4,000 sexual scenes and references each year on television. That's more than 38 a day. This information makes you want to place a few extra filters on the family computer!

Barna's research of sexual topics included the question: *Is it okay to enjoy sexual thoughts or fantasies?* According to the responses of people in a cross section of the United States, 59 percent believe it's okay to enjoy sexual thoughts and fantasies about having sexual relations. In the 18-21-year-old group, the average goes up to 79 percent who believe it is okay. And in the group of people 58 years and older, the average goes down to 40 percent. Now, that's quite a gap: 40 percent for those 58 years and older, and 79 percent for those 18-21 years of age.[2]

The above response is the reason I'm boldly speaking out about the hottest sex topics of the day. Our younger generation doesn't know and/or understand God's heart on the subject of sex!

What about having an abortion? Barna's cross-section statistics show that 45 percent of all Americans believe it is morally acceptable to have an abortion. Of the group who were 18-21 years old, 55 percent believe it's okay to have an abortion. But in the group 58 years and older, only 36 percent believe it's okay to have an abortion. Again, notice the difference. In the older group, the average is 36 percent, but in the younger group, the average is 55 percent.[3]

42 percent of the people in a cross section of America believe it's okay to have sex outside of marriage.

Again, we see our nation changing its view on a very important issue! What if that so called fetus is a real live baby? And I believe the Bible teaches us it is a life, a real baby. I'll do my best to prove this point further on in this book. Without a revelation of God's opinion, all restraints are off! We can justify the taking of a life in the name of a woman's rights, which I believe in so strongly. But none of us has the right to take a life, male or female!

On the question of having sex outside of marriage: 42 percent of the people in a cross section of America believe it's okay to have sex outside of marriage. In the 18-21-year-old group, 54 percent believe it's okay. But of those in the 58+ age group, only 24 percent believe it is okay. Notice the 30 percent difference between these two age groups.

What about looking at pornography of any kind—on the Internet, or any of the pay-per-view or premium channels on television? In a cross section of American survey participants, 38 percent believe it is okay. In the 18-21-year-old group, 50 percent believe it's okay. In the 58+ group, only 23 percent believe it's okay. Again, we find another huge percentage difference in the two age groups. Again, we see the restraints coming off!

What about the gay lifestyle? In a cross section of Americans, 30 percent believe the gay lifestyle is okay. In the 18-21-year-old group, the average goes up to 40 percent. And in the 58+ group, the average drops to 14 percent. Again, there is a wide gap between the two age groups.[4]

What makes the difference between these two groups? I believe this gap is the result of the younger generation not having heard God's opinion about the matter. Those who grew up thirty years ago were taught the Ten Commandments and other Bible standards even in school, not to mention in church, and I believe that's why they had higher moral standards than we have today.

It is the responsibility of parents to teach and train our children in the way they should go. It is our job—and privilege—to provide accurate and godly information to guide our children in the right direction. Proverbs 22:6 tells us to "teach a child to choose the right path, and when he is older he will remain upon it" (TLB). Unless we teach and train our children at home and participate with them in a Bible-believing church, they won't have a standard by which to measure all the crazy things that will bombard them as they mature. Without a doubt, society is teaching them that free sex is okay. Only you can combat this assault of misinformation with the Bible truth.

If you are a younger reader, I urge you to pay attention to your parents and to follow their biblical guidance. God's opinion restrains us and helps us walk in right paths that are good for us instead of taking wrong paths that are bad for us. God created us, and He knows what's best for us. And when it comes to the subject of sex—the hottest sex topics of our day—God has plenty to say. So take time to find out God's opinion and allow Him to guide you in the right direction.

Ephesians 5:1-2 admonishes us to "be imitators of God, therefore, as dearly loved children and live a life of love, just as Christ loved us and gave himself up for us as a fragrant offering and sacrifice to God." These verses clearly tell us that God wants us to act and live as He lived. But we have neither the capacity nor the ability to do it unless we know what He thinks and what He has to say. Verse three goes on to say, "But among you [Christians] there must not be even **a hint of sexual immorality**, or of any kind of impurity, or of greed, because these are improper for God's holy people." This is good information about how we must live if we are to be called God's holy people. The way I read it, there is no allowance for even the smallest amount of sexual immorality, impurity, or greed. That doesn't leave any room for opposing views about sexual behavior.

When I refer to sexual immorality in this book, I am talking about any type of sexual sin that is in our world today. And when it comes to sexual sin—it's not just having intercourse, but God calls any kind of sexual sin outside of the marriage relationship sexual immorality—He says there must not be even a hint of it in the lives of Christians. Now, some who have lived a lifestyle that falls into God's "unacceptable for Christians" category for many years may wonder how they can ever clean up their lives and be holy before God. The good news is that He never asks us to do anything that we're not able to do—with His help. If God wants us to do something, He will see to it that we are able to do it. God wants us to move up to a higher level where we will be able to live, act, and do the things He wants us to do.

> God wants us to move up to a higher level where we will be able to live, act, and do the things He wants us to do.

Are you ready to do so? I'm ready to help take you there!

God's Opinion in Review
Chapter 1

▎ The words in the Bible came out of God's mouth—He is speaking to mankind through the pages of His Word. Certain men were chosen to write the books of the Bible, but the important thing to remember is that God inspired them.

▎ The Bible includes God's opinion and His plan concerning everything that has to do with you and all of mankind.

▎ It is important to realize that the truth in the Bible can be twisted to make it say whatever people want it to say. Interpreting Scripture is extremely serious business, but the Bible can be rightly divided.

▎ You need to check out the Bible for yourself and make sure you are being taught the truth.

▎ Where there is no revelation of the Bible, we feel free to cast off restraint.

▎ There is a connection between what is going on in our society today and the failure to teach Judeo-

Christian values in our homes, in public and private schools, and in some churches.

∎ The current generation is the first to grow up with point-and-click pornography on the Internet; almost 90 percent have viewed it online, and have seen nearly 4,000 sexual scenes and references a year on television. This generation does not know or understand God's opinion about sex.

∎ Unless children are trained at home and participate in a Bible-believing church, they won't have a standard by which to measure all the craziness in the world as they mature.

∎ When it comes to the subject of sex—the hottest sex topics of our day—God has plenty to say. Take time to discover His opinion and allow Him to guide you in the right direction. He wants to move us up to a higher level where we will be able to live, act, and do the things He wants us to do.

Electrifying Sex?

DOES GOD'S OPINION ABOUT sex within the marriage vows include *exciting, electrifying, sex?* I believe this is a question that many people ponder, especially those who haven't had much exposure to Bible teaching. I remember the opinion I had after I accepted Jesus as my Savior at 19 years of age. As I stated earlier, I knew sex outside of marriage was wrong and I decided not to practice it because of the Holy Spirit convicting me and then eventually discovering the Bible told me not to. Yet, deep in my heart, I felt I was giving something up, that I was sacrificing great sex for okay sex to please God. I couldn't imagine that sex within

CHAPTER 2

marriage could compare to the loose, free sex that I had learned about in porn magazines.

I pictured God as this cranky old man in heaven who basically just tolerated people who had sex. I assumed that He allowed it but really didn't want anyone to enjoy it too much. But as I grew and studied the Bible, I found out that God actually wants us to *enjoy* sex, that He created it to be electrifying within marriage! God is very open to the subject of sex because He created it, and since He created it, He had a purpose for it.

God is very open to the subject of sex because He created it.

I'm going to share an excerpt from a love story that includes some very explicit sexual content. So just keep in mind that this book could be rated PG-13. As you read this story, try to guess the source.

> *Kiss me—full on the mouth!*
> *Yes! For your love is better than wine,*
> *headier than your aromatic oils.*
> *Take me away with you! Let's run off together!*
> *Yes! For your love is better than vintage wine.*
> *Everyone loves you—of course! And why not?*
> *When my King-Lover lay down beside me,*
> *my fragrance filled the room.*
> *His head resting between my breasts—*

Your lips are jewel red,
  your mouth elegant and inviting,
… Your breasts are like fawns,
  twins of a gazelle…
The sweet, fragrant curves of your body,
  the soft, spiced contours of your flesh
Invite me, and I come. I stay
  until dawn breathes its light and night slips
  away.
… You've captured my heart, dear….
  You looked at me, and I fell in love.
  One look my way and I was hopelessly in love!
The kisses of your lips are honey, my love….
  Your full breasts are like sweet clusters of dates.
I say "I'm going to climb that palm tree!
  I'm going to caress its fruit!"
Oh yes! Your breasts
  will be clusters of sweet fruit to me,
Your breath clean and cool like fresh mint,
  your tongue and lips like the best wine.

That story is very explicit, and includes some words that you probably never thought you'd see in religious reading. So it may surprise you to know that I didn't find this story in a modern-day novel or magazine. It did not come from the script of "Desperate Housewives" or the latest romantic movie to hit the big screen. This is actually an excerpt from the Bible, written by King Solomon and found in the Song of Solomon Chapters 1, 4, and 7 from THE MESSAGE Bible. And based on those very descriptive words, I think we can easily conclude that God created sex to be thrilling and electrifying for married couples. He included these words in the Bible, so He must be pro-*great* sex.

Actually, God is pro-great sex—it was His creation, designed to be enjoyable and electrifying within the marriage relationship. The three reasons for which He created sex in marriage are:

1. To consummate the marriage.
2. To populate the earth.
3. For simple pleasure and enjoyment *within the marital union.*

That's right! For simple pleasure and enjoyment *within the marital union!* Let's take a look at further evidence that God wants us to have great, enjoyable, electrifying sex as married couples. Most of the book of Proverbs was also written by Solomon, who became the king of Israel after his father, David. One day as Solomon was offering up a sacrifice unto God, God appeared to Him and said, "Ask for whatever you want me to give you" (2 Chronicles 1:7). And Solomon, realizing his lack of wisdom for the task ahead of him, said, "Give me wisdom and knowledge, that I may lead this people, for who is able to govern this great people of yours?" (v.10). And the Bible tells us that God gave Solomon more wisdom than any person who ever walked on the planet except for Jesus.

In the book of Proverbs, Solomon wrote God-inspired scriptures of wise instruction. Chapter 5 specifically deals with sexual issues, so for the purposes of this book, we're looking at the section that lets us know God's intentions with regard to enjoying sex within the marital union!

> *Drink water from your own well—share your love only with your wife. Why spill the water of your springs in public, having sex with just anyone? You should reserve it for yourselves. Don't share it with strangers.* **Let your wife be a fountain of blessing for you.** *Rejoice in the wife of your youth. She is a loving doe, a graceful deer.* **Let her breasts satisfy you always.** <u>*May you always be captivated by her love.*</u> *Why be captivated, my son, with an immoral woman, or embrace the breasts of an adulterous woman? For the* LORD *sees clearly what a man does, examining every path he takes. An evil man is held captive by his own sins;*

they are ropes that catch and hold him. He
will die for lack of self-control; he will be lost
because of his incredible folly.

—Proverbs 5:15-23 NLT (emphasis mine)

In this passage, God tells us that sex is meant to be enjoyed between a husband and wife! A wife's breasts were meant to bring satisfaction to her husband! Yep, that's in the Catholic, Protestant, and Jewish versions of the Bible! God's plan is that husbands and wives would always be captivated by their love. The word *captivated* means "to be influenced by irresistible appeal." In the Hebrew, *captivated* means "intoxicated." Intoxicated, as we know, means to be under the control of a substance. The love between a husband and wife can be so good and electrifying that it intoxicates them! So God is telling us that He created marital love and sex to be exciting, electrifying, irresistible, and enjoyable.

> God is telling us that He created marital love and sex to be exciting, electrifying, irresistible, and enjoyable.

God is also reminding us, in this section of Scripture, that we should have one wife or husband and that we shouldn't fool around sexually outside that relationship. He did not share these things to make life boring but to save us great pain! Forbidden fruit once tasted will poison our lives. I've watched so many people be destroyed because of infidelity, both Christian and non-Christian alike! Sexual activity is a spiritual as well as a physical connection. When you have sex with someone outside of marriage you are going to set into motion spiritual connections that will entangle you and destroy your life over time. We'll talk about this spiritual connection in chapter three. I'll also share how you can break sexual bondage later in the book. There is hope and freedom for all of us!

In Genesis, we really discover the importance God placed on Adam having a mate and the sexual relationship he would have with her. God created the earth and all the animals, and then He said,

> *But for Adam no suitable helper was found. So the LORD God caused the man to fall into a deep sleep; and while he was sleeping, he took one of the man's ribs and closed up the place with flesh.* **Then the LORD God made a woman** *from the rib he had taken out of the man, and he brought her to the man. The man said,* **"This is now bone of my bones and flesh of my flesh; she shall be called 'woman,'** *for she was taken out of the man."*
>
> —Genesis 2:20-23 (emphasis mine)

Then God talks about a special "uniting."

> *For this reason a man will leave his father
> and mother **and be united to his wife,** and
> they **will become one flesh.** The man and
> his wife were both naked, and **they felt no
> shame.***
>
> —vv. 24-25 (emphasis mine)

These verses contain some valuable information. This woman wasn't created just so Adam could have a friend. God had a bigger and better plan, so He created Eve to be Adam's wife. The two of them were united in the first marriage ceremony to ever take place when God brought Eve to Adam and said, "For this reason a man will leave his father and mother and be united to his wife." That word *united* here refers to the marital relationship. God created man to be united with a woman in marriage and to "become one flesh."

In the Old Testament, *one flesh* always refers to sexual intercourse, and this is what God is alluding to in verse 24. He's saying, "I'm uniting a man and a woman, and they will become one flesh." In other words, they will have a sexual relationship with each other. And He ends the chapter by telling us that they were naked and felt no shame. So way back at the beginning, in Genesis chapter 2 when God created man, He was saying, "I made man and woman to be united in marriage and become one flesh. Yes, the sexual relationship is meant to consummate the marriage and populate the earth, but I also gave it to you for pure pleasure and enjoyment. It is a blessing—My gift to you—so enjoy each other sexually without shame." Imagine, no shame! God was the one who initiated the sexual act and Adam and Eve felt no guilt before God as they preformed it! Adam and Eve were enjoying the gift of sex, just as God intended.

Then entered the serpent—the devil himself.

When the tempter came on the scene, he made quick work of polluting paradise. After just a short interlude with Eve, talking about trees and fruit, the devil convinced her that, contrary to what God had told Adam (see Genesis 2:9), it would be okay to eat of the fruit of the tree of the knowledge of good and evil. So Eve ate the forbidden fruit first, and then she took some to Adam, who also ate it. And at that very moment, sin entered their flesh and they died spiritually, and were separated from God.

Genesis 3 records the beginning of sin and shame:

> *Then the man and his wife heard the sound of the LORD God as He was walking in the garden in the cool of the day, and **they hid from the LORD God** among the*

trees of the garden. But the LORD *God called
to the man, "Where are you?" He answered,
"I heard you in the garden, and I was afraid
because* **I was naked; so I hid.***" And he said,
"Who told you that you were naked? Have
you eaten from the tree that I commanded
you not to eat from?"*

—vv. 8-11 (emphasis mine)

Notice that after they sinned, they realized they were naked, and when they heard the voice of God, they were ashamed. Adam and Eve were hiding from God because shame had entered the soul of mankind, and it remains to this day. But, thank God, He sent Jesus to fix all that. Now every person who puts their trust in Him not only receives salvation for their soul and the promise of a home in heaven, but Jesus also washes away their shame. He comes to live on the inside of us. He recreates us on the inside and our goal is to retrain our mind, with His opinion, so we live it on the outside!

The devil went right into the Garden of Eden and began to deceive Adam and Eve with his lies. And when they believed his lies and disobeyed God, they were banished from paradise and life was forever changed.

Today the devil still attempts to pollute God's good gifts, and sex is one of those good gifts! He works over-time trying to convince people that sex in marriage isn't all there is—that sex outside of marriage is better and way more fun. He infiltrates our homes with his false presentation of what great sex is and where it can be found by way of television, movies, magazines, and all kinds of sexual sites on the Internet. He uses any tool he can find to make his appeal, especially to our vulnerable young people, trying to convince them that free sex is not just okay but best. The lack of knowledge of God's opinion on this subject gives the devil free reign to form mankind's opinion and to literally control us.

The devil is a brilliant strategist—he doesn't hit us with something big all at once. He enters slowly with his subtle lies or half truths at first, and then they begin to grow and increase until sexual sin is widespread. It becomes the norm and Christian views are soon seen as outdated and archaic. Good-hearted people are programmed with all of this misinformation and believe something that is contrary to God's point of view, without realizing it. This is what happened in Bible days. Sexual sin became so rampant that God had to literally send a flood to destroy the uncontrolled sin that was on the earth.

He wants people who are bound by sexual sin to find freedom and follow His plan.

Our world is again afflicted with out-of-control sin, including sexual sin, and I believe God wants to send a flood of His Word to help people clean up their acts. He wants people who are bound by sexual sin to find freedom and follow His plan, which is to enjoy really, really, great electrifying sex, *within the marital relationship*—not outside it. I ran across a very interesting article on the Internet while doing the research for this book. It turned out to be what was referred to as "a landmark study" by researchers based at The University of Chicago in 1994. It disputes many myths about sexual behavior in America. "The study involved 90-minute, face-to-face interviews with 3,432 randomly selected Americans ages 18 to 59. Because the questionnaire included a number of cross checks on the respondents' veracity, the investigators have much confidence that the data provide accurate estimates for such sensitive behavior as sexual practices and preferences, extramarital sex, number of sexual partners and homosexuality," according to the *University of Chicago Chronicle*, October 13, 1994, volume 14, number 4.[1]

The Chronicle quotes the study which was published in a book entitled *Sex in America* by Little, Brown and Co. of New York, and I quote, "The researchers say their findings will help Americans deal with such questions as: How should we combat the spread of AIDS? Would punitive policies reduce the number of abortions? Why are teenagers having sex? Is marriage on its way out?"[2]

"The results reveal an important new way of thinking about sexuality. Sexual behavior is not just determined by instinct, the investigators argue, but is socially determined and socially controlled to a greater extent than previously believed. Friends, family, neighborhoods, religious beliefs and education dramatically influence who Americans choose for sexual partners, how many partners they have and how they behave sexually. The study finds that Americans have less sex, fewer partners and less erotic sex than other, less reliable studies have indicated."[3]

> Sexual behavior... is socially determined and socially controlled to a greater extent than previously believed.

Among the findings of the study are the following:

1. Americans have sex about once a week, on average.
2. A third of adult Americans have sex a few times a year or not at all.
3. The median number of sexual partners in a lifetime for American men is six.
4. For women, the median number is two.
5. More than 80 percent of Americans had only one partner or no partner in the past year and just 3 percent of women and men had five or more partners in the past year.
6. Marriage is alive and well. Almost all Americans marry, and 75 percent of married

men and 85 percent of married women say they have remained faithful.

7. The people who have the most sex and are happiest with their sex lives are monogamous couples.

8. Geography plays an important role in the formation of homosexual communities. About 9 percent of the men and 3 percent of the women living in the nation's largest cities identify themselves as homosexual or bisexual.

9. The reasons cited for teenage girls having sex for the first time has changed over the decades. In previous generations, most women said they had sex for the first time because of affection for their partner, and only 13 percent said the reason was peer pressure. In contrast, 37 percent of the younger women who participated in the survey said the reason they had sex for the first time was peer pressure, and only 35 percent said it was out of affection for their partner.

10. Depending on how the question was asked, people have a variety of responses on their sexual preferences. Five percent of men report having had a sexual encounter with another man as an adult, while 2.8 percent

say they are homosexual or bisexual. Four percent of women report having had a sexual encounter with another woman as an adult, while 1.5 say they are homosexual or bisexual.[4]

Particularly notice point 7. How often do we hear anything at all about the benefits of traditional marriage, and how the best sex is in a traditional marital setting, between one man and one woman impacting our society? Yet Dr. James Dobson's *Focus on the Family's* Web site article "Why Marriage Matters" states:

"Researchers are finding that marriage has a much greater impact in our lives than many have assumed. This is especially true in the area of adult health and well-being. Sociologist Linda Waite and researcher Maggie Gallagher explain, 'the evidence from four decades of research is surprisingly clear: a good marriage is both men's and women's best bet for living a long and healthy life.' Men and women who are in their first marriages, on average, enjoy significantly higher levels of physical and mental health than those who are either single, divorced or living together."[5]

This same article quotes a leading social scientist, James Q. Wilson as follows: "Married people are happier than unmarried ones of the same age, not only in the United States, but in at least seventeen other countries where similar inquiries have been made. And there seems to be good reasons for that happiness. People who are married not only have higher incomes and enjoy greater emotional support, they tend to be healthier. Married people live longer than unmarried ones, not only in the United States but abroad."[6]

The media would have us believe that the best and most satisfying sex happens between two Hollywood "hotties."

The media would have us believe that the best and most satisfying sex happens between two Hollywood "hotties." They are portrayed as the "beautiful people" with the sexiest bodies and, of course, their sexual experience would have to be the best and most satisfying! But we know, from the Bible, that this isn't true. And a survey conducted more than a decade ago by a secular university confirmed it. The results of their survey show that **the average husband and wife who marry as virgins and remain monogamous**—you know, a little bit overweight, maybe not extremely handsome or beautiful—**have the best and most satisfying sex.**[7] Isn't that exciting?

Some people think, *Well, I must be missing something. If I could just have a one-night stand, maybe I would really experience sexual pleasure like I've never experienced before.* Well, there is pleasure in most sexual activity, but when it comes to being satisfied and truly enjoying an electrifying experience day after day, husbands and wives win.

The study further concluded: **"The highest level of sexual satisfaction is between married conservative Christians."**[8] Whoa! This is remarkable. The survey done by the University of Chicago concluded that the highest level of sexual satisfaction is between married, conservative Christians. Most people think we live these boring lives and that we have sex just to have babies, but this survey says otherwise. If people knew and understood these facts they'd stay married and get some religion real fast!

The world is trying to convince us that there's something better out there, and that's why so many men and even some women are bound by pornography. They think there must be something outside of their frame of reference that's better than they have. As a person who was deeply involved in pornography and sexual activity before I was married and before I met Christ, I can tell you that I was never satisfied and that there is no one better than your own mate! It's true, God made sex to be enjoyable, electrifying, and satisfying. The world is discovering that this happens in a monogamous marital relationship—and it's at its best and highest level in a conservative Christian relationship. That makes you want to pause and say, "Thank You, Jesus!" Yes, God's okay with us enjoying sex!

A similar study was done by the Family Research Council of Washington, D.C. They found that **72 percent of married traditionalists reported sexual satisfaction.** This means that traditionalists who are in a normal male and female marriage reported sexual satisfaction. This is 31 percent higher than unmarried non-traditionalists who are active sexually. So of the married traditionalists who were surveyed, 72 percent said they have sexual satisfaction, but only 41 percent of the unmarried non-traditionalists surveyed could say that.[9] The study also concluded that sexually happy people also tend to go to church. Some two-thirds of the responders who attend church weekly are very satisfied with their sex lives, compared to barely half of those who never attend church. Why not go to church tonight? It will probably improve your sex life!

God is painting a picture for us, and He is saying, "Listen up! I created sex to be enjoyed within the marital relationship, not outside of it." The University of Chicago survey confirms that the best and most enjoyable sex is between husbands and wives who are married to each other.

The apostle Paul also addressed this issue:

> *Now, getting down to the questions you asked in your letter to me. First, is it a good thing to have sexual relations? Certainly—**but only within a certain***

*context. It's good for a man to have a wife, and for a woman to have a husband. Sexual drives are strong, but marriage is strong enough to contain them **and provide for a balanced and fulfilling sexual life** in a world of sexual disorder.*
—1 Corinthians 7:1-2, THE MESSAGE (emphasis mine)

A *world of sexual disorder*—isn't that an accurate description of our world today? Yet in the midst of such disorder, the Bible tells us that the marriage relationship is strong enough to overcome it and provide a balanced and fulfilling sexual life. That is good news in a world full of bad news. Isn't it good to know God's opinion regarding the hottest sex topics of our day? What a blessing to know that God created sex to be fun, enjoyable, and fulfilling within the marriage relationship.

> What a blessing to know that God created sex to be fun, enjoyable, and fulfilling within the marriage relationship.

I wish the media portrayed these facts about sex and marriage, but they don't. It's up to us to make sure our children understand that the best sex is inside the marital union! We must make sure they understand that what they're seeing and hearing on television is not reality!

Clearly, married people have the best sex!

God's Opinion in Review
Chapter 2

▌ God actually wants us to enjoy exciting, electrifying sex within marriage. He is very open to the subject of sex because He created it!

▌ Three reasons for which God created sex are: (1) To consummate the marriage; (2) To populate the earth; and (3) For simple pleasure and enjoyment within the marriage union.

▌ God reminds us in Scripture that we should have one wife or husband and that we shouldn't fool around sexually outside that relationship. He did not share these things to make life boring, but to save us great pain.

▌ God didn't create Eve to be Adam's friend. The Bible says that when God brought Eve to Adam, it was for the purpose of uniting them. Uniting a man and woman is referring to marriage. God then goes on to say that they shall become one flesh, which is referring to intercourse.

▌ When the devil showed up, he polluted paradise. Sin and shame instantly became associated with sex.

■ A lack of knowledge of God's opinion on the subject of sex gives the devil free reign to form mankind's opinion and to literally control us. Thus, our world is afflicted with out-of-control sin, including sexual sin, as in the days of Noah and the Flood, and God wants to send a flood of His Word to help people clean up their acts.

■ The highest level of sexual satisfaction is between married, conservative Christians.

■ In a world of sexual disorder, the marriage relationship remains strong. What a blessing to know that God created sex to be fun, enjoyable, electrifying, and fulfilling within the marriage relationship— information we will never learn from watching television.

Single Sex?

MANY YOUNG PEOPLE TODAY ARE confused about what is right and wrong with regard to sexual relationships. If they believe what they see and hear all around them about sex, they probably believe that "anything goes" outside of marriage. I feel for them because they're dealing with the highest hormone levels they'll ever experience, the mystery of what having sex will be like, and the bombardment of the ideologies of free and wild sex outside of marriage. Talk about adversity! On top of all these things, I can't lie to young people or adults and tell them that sex isn't fun outside of marriage. Initially, it is. And because it's "forbidden fruit," it seems even more attractive. I can tell them, however, that the fun only lasts for minutes and afterward—especially years down the road—they'll wish they'd known God's opinion and had followed it. Also, remember what we learned in chapter two: The most fulfilling and fun sex is within the marital union.

I wish I had known more about God's opinion when I was a teenager. I was involved in sexual activity from a very young age, like 10 or 11. When I accepted Christ at the age of nineteen, I immediately knew that sexual activity outside of marriage was wrong, but I struggled with resisting it. Even when I found out what God had

> We must find out what God considers to be sexual sin.

to say about sex, I continued to struggle, trying to free myself from my sexual involvement. It wasn't easy, but as I prayed and studied the Bible, God taught me how to work His principles in my life so I could walk free in that area. I'll teach you those principles later in this book.

Is it okay for single people to have sex? To answer this question we must first find out what God considers to be sexual sin. Is it just intercourse, or are there other things that people can get away with? Is foreplay okay? Are there other sex acts that are acceptable? Or does God want singles to stay away from all those things? Allow me to paint a picture for you of what's taking place in the world in which we currently live.

Lauren Winner, the author of *Real Sex: The Naked Truth about Chastity*, has this to say: "In 2003, researchers at Northern Kentucky University showed that 61 percent of students who signed sexual abstinence commitment cards broke their pledges. Of the remaining 49 percent who kept their pledges, 55 percent said they had oral sex and did not consider oral sex to be a sin."[1]

The Center for Disease Control reports that: "In the United States in 2005, 47 percent of high school students had had sexual intercourse, and 14 percent of high school students had had four or more sex partners during their life."[2]

According to the Alan Guttmacher Institute, "most young people have sex for the first time at about age 17."[3]

The University of Chicago Chronicle reviewed a book released in 2001 called, *Sex, Love, and Health in America: Private Choices and Public Policies.* Coeditors Edward O. Laumann and Robert T. Michael found that "Over the past half century there has been no trend in the birth rate rising among teenagers under age 18: about 10 percent of teenage women in each recent decade have had a baby by the time they turn 18. What has changed dramatically is the rate at which teen women engage in sex before age 18. Forty years ago, 29 percent engaged in sex before age 18, compared to 63 percent recently. The data also indicates that this has been offset by both a greater use of more effective contraceptives

(25 percent used contraception during their first sex act 40 years ago compared to 40 percent recently) and an increase in the use of abortion (a tiny percentage 40 years ago compared to 27 percent of teenagers recently)." Can you imagine that 6 out of 10 high school students are sexually active? Can you imagine that 27 percent of teenage girls have an abortion? This information makes me glad that we've raised our children to understand God's mercy, love, and opinion concerning sex! Otherwise I'd lock my girls up until they were 25 or so. Because of how they were raised, I trust my children to resist temptation and make the correct choices.

They also report the consequences of the sexual revolution of the late 1960s. The study documents considerable "erosion of organized religion and middle-class status in organizing people's sexual lives in the wake of the Sexual Revolution. Before 1970, being raised Catholic or having a middle-class mother played a substantial role in reducing a woman's likelihood of having sex before age 18. Now the principle factors affecting that decision are having an intact family (both biological parents present) when aged 14, late age of menarche, and not having had a sexual experience before the age of sexual maturity. Over the past several decades there has been a trend toward more similarity between men and women in the age at which they first have sex as well as a dramatic increase in the rates of premarital sex."[4]

Society has programmed young and old alike to believe they're not having sex unless they're having intercourse. In fact, "Nowadays girls don't consider oral sex to be sex. It's just "something to do." Another said, "It's no big deal," in an *Atlantic Weekly* article, dated Tuesday, January 17, 2006.

A *U.S. News & World Report* article, dated April 4, 2005, reported a University of California-San Francisco study conducted to assess teens' attitudes and behavior toward oral sex.

"What they wanted to know: *How often do young teens have oral sex, and do they perceive it as a risky thing to do?*

"What they found after surveying 580 ninth graders at two California public high schools, 58 percent of whom were female: About 20 percent of the students reported having had oral sex, compared with 14 percent who said they'd had intercourse. In addition, nearly one third of the students said they planned on having oral sex within the next six months, as compared with only a quarter of the students who planned to have intercourse. Teens, on average, said oral sex carries fewer health and emotional risks and is more socially acceptable than intercourse. They said that more of their peers were having and were likely to have oral sex than intercourse."

"What it means to [us as a society]: Though studies and sex education classes focus on intercourse, this report shows that teens are more likely to engage in oral sex and consider it less risky and more socially acceptable. The authors [of the study] say that people who work with young people need to include discussion of oral sex in education and counseling."

The article continued, "Although with oral sex there's no risk of pregnancy, there is still a substantial risk of contracting a sexually transmitted disease, including herpes, Chlamydia, and even HIV."[5]

Young people are experiencing the highest level of hormones raging through their bodies that they will ever experience.

What is God's opinion about all this? What is allowed and not allowed when it comes to sexual activity? Is it okay to go so far and then stop? Or does God want singles to avoid all of it?

Young people—not just teens but people in their 20s—as discussed at the beginning of this chapter are experiencing the highest level of hormones raging through their bodies that they will ever experience in their lives. What are they supposed to do? They are fully developed physically, and the hormones are kicking in big time. It's kind of like being all dressed up with nowhere to go when somebody says, "Hey, sex is just for marriage and that's it." And, as we already discussed, the world they live in is flooding them with images that tell them it's okay to enjoy sex outside of marriage. Is that what God says?

Let's begin to examine God's opinion on what sex is and isn't and if it is all right outside of marriage.

> *Finally then, brethren, we urge and exhort in the Lord Jesus that you should abound more and more, just as you received from us how you ought to walk and to please God; for you know what commandments we gave you through the Lord Jesus.* **For this is the will of God,** *your sanctification* [growing in holiness]: *that* **you should abstain from sexual immorality;** *that each of you should know how to possess his own vessel in sanctification and honor, not in passion of lust, like the Gentiles who do not know God; that no one should take advantage of and defraud his brother* **in this matter** [sexual immorality], *because the Lord is the avenger of all such, as we also forewarned you and testified. For God did not call us* **to uncleanness** [sexual immorality in this context], *but in holiness. Therefore he who*

rejects this [avoiding sexual immorality]
*does **not reject man, but God**, who has also*
given us His Holy Spirit.
—1 Thessalonians 4:1-8 NKJV
(emphasis mine)

Here, the apostle Paul is saying, "I taught you how
to live as Christians, and you are doing pretty well, but
I'd like to see you do even better." Then he goes on to
say, "For you know what charges and precepts we gave
you [on the authority and by the inspiration of] the
Lord Jesus. For this is the will of God, that you should
be consecrated (separated and set apart for pure and
holy living): that you should abstain and shrink from
all sexual vice" (vv. 2-3) as the Amplified Bible puts it.
These verses tell us that God wants us to abstain—to
run away from—all sexual vice. And in verse 3, Paul
says, "This is the will of God." The Bible says if we don't
take this advice we're not rejecting Pastor Joe or some
other Christian leader, but God! This is God's opinion:
stay away from sexual activity! Let's make sure you
understand that this isn't referring to just intercourse.

In chapter 3 of his book, *Sanctity of Life,* author
Charles Swindoll, referring to those instructions to
the Thessalonians, writes: "How broad is this word for
sexual immorality? It is the Greek term *porneia* which
includes homosexuality, incestuous relationships,

unnatural acts with beasts and animals, premarital sexual relationships and extramarital sex."[6]

From the Greek word *porneia*, we derive our English word *pornography*, which *Strong's Greek Dictionary of the New Testament* defines as "harlotry; also fornication; uncleanness; idolatry; adultery; incest."[7] In other words, this word is referring to any kind of sexual activity—in the mind, the heart, or physically. It doesn't refer just to intercourse, but it could mean intercourse. It could also refer to homosexuality, fantasizing while viewing pornography on the Internet or television, or any other sexual sin. Notice that God says we should shrink from or abstain from all sexual vice—*porneia*. So in God's opinion—the only opinion that really should matter to a Christian—these things are wrong, and God wants us to stay away from them.

There's another scripture in the book of Ezekiel where God is speaking to a backslidden Israel. These people were serving other gods, and they didn't want anything to do with the living God. So He compares their backslidden state to a married person who is in an adulterous affair. God often compares being backslidden—going after the world and making it number one instead of Him—to sexual sin. And in this scripture—a very graphic PG-13 scripture—He shows us that just petting and touching certain parts of the body are considered sexual sin and they are wrong. Now, sex is more than body parts—more than an attractive guy or a cute girl. It's more than just a prince charming coming in to sweep the princess off her feet. God created sex to be the most fun and rewarding event—but He created it to be enjoyed within the marital relationship. It's not designed for singles, although they'll feel the desires rising in them to have sex, which are natural, but they must be fought off until marriage.

Ezekiel penned these God-inspired words,

> God's Message came to me: "Son of man, there were two women, daughters of the same mother. They became whores in Egypt, whores from a young age. **Their breasts were fondled, their young bosoms caressed.**"
> —Ezekiel 23:1-3 THE MESSAGE
> (emphasis mine)

Notice that God considers touching in a sexual way to be sin. It is His opinion that touching, petting, and caressing are sexual sins. It is so unacceptable to Him that in this verse, He speaks strongly, calling the girls "whores." I realize that all kinds of sexual behavior are acceptable in today's world, but God does not find it acceptable. To Him it is sin, and He hates sin. As I've already said, there was a time in my life when I lived in that kind of sin and thought it was okay. The world I lived in as a young teenager said it was okay as long as nobody knew about it and no one would be hurt by it. And since I had never heard what the Bible said about it, I didn't recognize it was wrong to participate in sexual activity of every kind.

As I mentioned earlier, when I accepted Christ as my Savior and allowed God to come into my life, He made me aware of what was wrong—sin. He made me aware that I could and should resist it! I also discovered that even though God hates sin, He loves sinners. He eagerly waits for us to repent and accept Christ so He can extend His life-changing freedom to us! He'll do the same for anyone who trusts in Him!

The Bible includes several other Scriptures that prove sex outside of marriage is wrong in God's eyes. He created sex for marital relationships, and when single people participate in sex outside of marriage, they sadden our heavenly Father.

> *When single people participate in sex outside of marriage, they sadden our heavenly Father.*

Flee from sexual immorality [sexual sin of any kind]. *All other sins a man commits are outside his body, but he who sins sexually sins against his own body. Do you not know that your body is a temple of the Holy Spirit, who is in you, whom you have received from God? You are not your own; you were bought at a price. Therefore* **honor God** *with your body* [avoiding sexual sin is one way we honor God with our bodies. This is the context referred to in this section of Scriptures].

—1 Corinthians 6:18-20 (emphasis mine)

God's instruction to us is to flee any type of sexual sin. This is for our own good, as we'll discover shortly. I think we all know what it means to flee! God wants us to run from sexual sin as we would run from a nuclear bomb that has one hour left on the timer! How fast would you move in the opposite direction of that nuclear bomb? Would you flee? I think so! That's how quickly you should flee from sexual sin! First Corinthians 6:18-20 also teaches us that we will honor and please God if we avoid having sex outside of marriage. The last thing that I want to do, and I'm sure you agree, is to displease God! I truly want to honor Him! Let's take a look at some further evidence of God's opinion on this subject.

Now for the matters you wrote about: It is good for a man not to marry. But since there is so much **immorality** [sexual sin of any kind outside of marriage], *each man should have his own wife, and each woman her own husband. The husband should* **fulfill his marital duty** [having sex] *to his wife, and likewise the wife* [having sex] *to her husband. The wife's body does not belong to her alone but also to her husband. In the same way, the husband's body does not belong to him alone but also to his wife.* **Do not deprive each other** [of sex] *except by mutual consent and for a time, so that you may devote yourselves to prayer.* **Then come together** [have sex with one another] *again so that Satan will not tempt you because of your lack of self-control.*

    —1 Corinthians 7:1-5 (emphasis mine)

We learn many key truths about marriage and sex in these verses from Corinthians. The context of this letter is very important in understanding why the Bible would say it's not good for a man or women to marry. The Corinthian Christians were living in difficult times—actually being severely persecuted. It was Paul's opinion—not necessarily the Lord's opinion—that men would only experience additional heartache if they had a wife and children to worry about. These verses aren't applicable for those of us living in the U.S. or much of today's world. Without a doubt, God is teaching in this text that sex is not for singles. He clearly says that we should marry so we don't sin sexually!

I think all these scriptures make it very clear that God doesn't want us to be involved in sexual relationships outside of marriage.

Being sexually involved outside of marriage, even when you're married, creates three serious problems:

1. It separates you from having intimacy with the God.
2. It clouds the minds of the sexual partners, creating confusion that makes it difficult to make decisions.
3. It affects intimacy with your current mate or your mate when you get married.

Practicing sex outside of marriage or having an affair will separate you from God! All sin will separate us from God. Any time we disobey what the Bible says, we put up a wall between us and God. Thank God we can repent of sin and tear that wall down! Sexual activity outside of the marriage union also brings confusion and will affect your intimacy in this area when you do get married. Again, thank God we can repent and He'll cleanse us and fix those problems! I believe that confusion comes and intimacy is affected because sex is as much a spiritual act as a physical act.

> *There's **more to sex** <u>than mere skin on skin</u>. Sex is as much **spiritual mystery** as physical fact. As written in Scripture, "The two become one." Since we want to become spiritually one with the Master, we must not pursue the kind of sex that avoids commitment and intimacy, leaving us **more lonely than ever**—the kind of sex that can never "become one."*
>
> —1 Corinthians 6:16-17 THE MESSAGE
> (emphasis mine)

This passage lets us know that when a man and woman have a sexual relationship in marriage, the two become one. There's something spiritual about a sexual relationship in marriage. Commitment here refers to marriage, and intimacy refers to a very close, exclusive, and special relationship. The world tries to tell us that sex is just a physical relationship involving body parts, and sex *is* physical. Verse 16 confirms that. But it takes intimacy and commitment to have a fulfilling sexual relationship, as confirmed by the aforementioned Chicago University survey. Their results concluded that born-again conservative Christians have the most satisfying sexual relationships of all the people surveyed.[9] Do you know why? It is because God created it for the intimacy of marriage. It's as much spiritual as it is physical! Those who become involved in sexual activity outside of marriage miss out on intimacy and bring a cloud of confusion in their lives because this is also a spiritual act meant to involve only your mate. I cannot stress enough that unless they seek forgiveness and healing, their past sexual experiences will affect, and perhaps ruin, their sexual intimacy when they do marry. God is able and willing to deliver anyone from their sexual "baggage." They simply have to repent from the heart!

The Bible says:

> *Honor marriage, and guard* **the sacredness of sexual intimacy** *between wife and husband.* <u>*God draws a firm line against casual and illicit sex*</u> [any type of sexual activity outside of marriage].
>
> —Hebrews 13:4 THE MESSAGE
> (emphasis mine)

Honoring marriage—both our own and the marriages of others—must be a high priority to us. Sex isn't just sex, it is sacred. This means it is a holy activity created by God for marriage only. Again, the Bible makes God's opinion very clear when it comes to sexual activity outside of marriage. He created it for marriage.

There is also a natural problem that having sex outside of marriage can cause: Sexually transmitted diseases. Some Christians believe that STDs are God's judgment on those who have sex outside of marriage, and maybe they are. Honestly, I'm not sure. I can say that they are the result of sexual loose living, which should also speak to us that God created sex for the marital union. I was amazed as I researched the upcoming facts. These alone would keep me from having sex outside of marriage if I was single and not a Christian. Sex outside of marriage is dangerous!

"Sexually transmitted diseases (STDs) remain a major public health challenge in the United States. While substantial progress has been made in preventing, diagnosing, and treating certain STDs in recent years, CDC estimates that 19 million new infections occur each year, almost half of them among young people ages 15 to 24."[10] Wow! These are some inconceivable statistics, and as I said before, even if you didn't care what God said—it's hard to have safe sex. I believe the number-one reason for abstaining from sexual relationships outside of marriage should be to

> The number-one reason for abstaining from sexual relationships outside of marriage should be to obey and please God.

obey and please God. But beyond that, I think it is very wise to remain sexually pure for your own personal protection.

Groaning in anguish when disease consumes your body

We looked at Proverbs 5 in chapter two. It is a strong warning against having sex outside of marriage that clearly spells out what can happen to your life. Verse 11 mentions "...you will groan in anguish when disease consumes your body" (NLT). Again, this doesn't mean it is God's judgment. He is, however, warning us that sex outside of marriage will bring diseases. It's like us telling our children, "Don't put your hand in the fire—it will burn you!" If they should put their hand in the fire and be burned, is that the result of our judgment or a natural consequence for defying a natural law? Again, I can't say with confidence that it's a specific judgment that God is aiming toward an individual. On the other hand, will God judge us for sins we didn't repent of when we're at His judgment seat in heaven? Yes!

The Center for Disease Control and Prevention based in Atlanta, GA, is a division of the U.S. Department of Health and Human Services. Their "Sexually Transmitted Disease Surveillance 2005" report summarizes 2005 national data on trends in notifiable STDs—Chlamydia, gonorrhea, and syphilis.

"Chlamydia remains the most commonly reported infectious disease in the United States. In 2005, 976,445 Chlamydia diagnoses were reported, up from 929,462 in 2004. Even so, most Chlamydia cases go undiagnosed. It is estimated that there are approximately 2.8 million new cases of Chlamydia in the U.S. each year.

"Young women are hardest hit by this disease," according to the report, "and the long-term consequences of Chlamydia are much more severe for women. It causes pelvic inflammatory disease (PID), ectopic pregnancy, and up to 20 percent of those untreated for Chlamydia experience infertility.

"Gonorrhea is the second most commonly reported infectious disease in the U.S., with 339,593 cases reported in 2005. The gonorrhea rate in 2005 was 115.6 cases per 100,000 population. It remains substantially under-diagnosed and under-reported, and approximately twice as many new infections are estimated to occur each year as are reported. Drug resistance is an increasingly important concern in the treatment and prevention of gonorrhea."

I want you to grasp how alarming these statistics are. Not only are these diseases on the rise among our young people, but treatment of these very serious illnesses are not working.

What the CDC described next was even more startling. "Syphilis cases have increased for the fifth consecutive year. The rate of primary and secondary (P&S) syphilis—the most infectious stages of the disease—decreased throughout the 1990s, reaching an all-time low in 2000. However, over the past five years, the rate has begun to steadily increase with a substantial increase of incidence in males (from 4.7 per 100,000 population in 2004 to 5.1 in 2005).

"Troubling trends were also seen among females, as the rate of reported cases increased for the first time in more than ten years. And the rate of P&S syphilis among males is now six times the rate among women." They believe the rising rates are driven largely by cases among men who have sex with men.

"Syphilis, a highly infectious genital ulcerative disease is easily curable in its early (primary and secondary) stages. Untreated, however, it can lead to serious long-term complications such as neurological, cardiovascular, organ damage, and even death. Congenital syphilis can cause stillbirth, death soon after birth, and physical deformity and neurological complications in children who survive. Like many other STDs, syphilis facilitates the spread of HIV, increasing transmission of the virus at least two- to five-fold."[11]

You just can't go wrong by obeying God in all things—including His admonitions regarding sexual relationships.

You just can't go wrong by obeying God in all things—including His admonitions regarding sexual relationships. So whether you're married or single, remember: "God draws a firm line against casual and illicit sex." Obey Him and keep yourself pure so you can one day enjoy the ultimate intimacy of the marriage relationship. What is the best way to communicate the truth of God's opinion about why sexual purity matters?

Focus on the Family recruited a team of Bible scholars in May 2000 to develop a Bible-based statement on sexual behavior. They called it the Colorado Statement on Biblical Sexual Morality. Their hope is that the foundational bodies listed here will work in concert to admonish young people about sexual purity:

- *Local Churches and Pastors* need to preach the truth (that any sex outside of marriage is sin) in love (remembering that God has a tremendous capacity to forgive repentant sinners.)
- *Seminaries (Bible schools)* need to prepare church leaders to resist sexual temptations and to give Bible-based compassionate counsel to those who have fallen.
- *Parachurch Ministries* that specifically promote sexual abstinence until marriage and marital fidelity need to work together.

❱ *Parents* must recognize that they are the most significant influences in their children's lives. They need to model and teach strong, loving, faithful marriages to children.[12]

In closing this chapter, allow me to share the true story of A.C. Green, a former NBA basketball star who played for the Los Angeles Lakers, the Phoenix Suns, the Dallas Mavericks, and ended his successful career with the Miami Heat. He is now a youth mentor, author, speaker, and successful businessman. He is also a role model whom youth across America can respect. His main focus is sexual abstinence education.

NBA Iron Man, A.C. (not initials standing for his real name—A.C. is his real name) Green became famous not only as a forward for the Lakers for eight seasons and for playing in 1,192 straight games, but because of his stand for sexual abstinence until he married. Once one of the NBA's most eligible bachelors, A.C. Green married his beautiful wife in April 2002, at the age of 38. And when he was asked after his wedding about his life-long vow to purity until marriage, he said, "It was worth the wait."[13]

With all of the unimaginable temptation presented to professional athletes, it is good to see an NBA star who stayed pure sexually and said it was worth the wait. To that, I say, "Amen! Thank you for a great example to follow, A.C."

God's Opinion in Review
Chapter 3

■ A University of Chicago study reveals that the rate at which teen women engage in sex before age 18 has increased dramatically. Six out of ten high school students are sexually active and 27 percent of teenage girls have had an abortion. The study also reports that the 1960s sexual revolution initiated the erosion of organized religion and middle-class status in organizing people's sexual lives.

■ Nowadays neither teens nor adults consider oral sex to be sex. It's just "something to do." These trends show that sex education classes, which now focus on intercourse, need to inform teens that oral sex may be more socially acceptable, but it still provides a substantial risk of contracting sexually transmitted diseases, such as herpes, Chlamydia, and even HIV.

■ With hormones raging at their peak, young singles must be exposed to God's opinion on what sex is and isn't and that it isn't acceptable to God outside of marriage. God's opinion says (not merely suggests) staying away from sexual activity.

▌ Being sexually involved outside of marriage creates three problems: (1) It separates you from having intimacy with God; (2) It clouds the minds of sexual partners, creating confusion that makes decisions difficult; (3) It affects intimacy with your current or future lifetime mate.

▌ There is something spiritual about a sexual relationship in marriage. Commitment refers to marriage, and intimacy refers to a very close, exclusive, and special relationship. Sex is physical, of course, but it takes intimacy and commitment to have a fulfilling sexual relationship. It's as much spiritual as it is physical.

▌ Proverbs 5:2 contains a strong warning against having sex outside of marriage that can result in "anguishing diseases consuming your body." Although many consider STDs God's judgment, it is simply a fact that if you play with fire, you will be burned.

▌ The Center for Disease Control and Prevention reports that Chlamydia remains the most commonly reported infectious disease in the U.S., with an estimated 2.8 million new cases annually. This disease alone can cause pelvic inflammatory disease, ectopic pregnancy, and infertility. Gonorrhea and syphilis cases are increasing.

▮ Obey God and keep yourself pure so you can one day enjoy the ultimate intimacy of the marriage relationship.

▮ Local churches and pastors must preach the truth; seminaries and Bible schools should prepare leaders to resist sexual temptation and provide compassionate counsel to those who have fallen. Parachurch ministries must promote sexual abstinence and marital fidelity. Parents must recognize who is influencing their children and model strong, loving, faithful marriages to children.

▮ Motivate your children to model mentors like NBA basketball star, A.C. Green, who was asked after his wedding about his life-long vow to purity until marriage. His response? "It was worth the wait."

Porn & Mental Sex?

I N CONSIDERING THE "RIGHTS AND wrongs" of sexual behavior, fantasizing (sex in the mind—often with the help of pornography) is a hot topic these days. Many people have heard so many different opinions that they are asking, "Is sexual fantasizing really a sin? Is it possible to sin in the mind and heart?" In order to answer these questions, we need to know God's standard, and His standard is clearly recorded in the Bible. In this chapter, we will be considering some statistics and looking into God's opinion on the subject.

There is so much pornographic material available today that fantasizing about sexual things is a bigger problem than ever before.

weekly news program aired a story in 2003 reporting that well over 800 million adult videotapes and DVDs were rented in video stores across the country. Imagine how many more there are today! These products no longer have to be picked up at the video store because they can now be downloaded onto home computers. The nation's largest cable company pulled in $50 million from adult programming more than five years ago, and all the nation's top cable operators distribute sexually explicit material to their subscribers. But you won't read about it in their annual reports, and it's the same with satellite providers.

Christians and even pastors are giving in to this insidious temptation. "In an August, 2000 survey of its readership by *Christianity Today* magazine, 36 percent of laymen responding have visited a sexually explicit Internet site, of which 44 percent have visited such sites 'a few times' in the past year."[1] "In a 2002 survey of 6,000 pastors visiting the website of Saddleback Community Church in Mission Viejo, CA, 30 percent admitted viewing Internet pornography in the last 30 days."[2]

My intent in sharing this information is not to put down pastors who are trying to serve God. The point I want to make is that if pastors are struggling at this level, then where are the rest of Americans in their struggle with porn?

In his book, *Every Man's Battle*, Steve Arterburn says 10 percent of men have sexual addictions, and 10 percent of men are never tempted at all. This means that 10 percent of them are so addicted to it that they can't stop—they have to have it every day. The other 10 percent don't care about sex (this may just be me, but perhaps they have a hormone deficiency or something like that). Arterburn says that the other 80 percent live in various shades of gray when it comes to sexual sin.[3] They are involved at different levels and they think at different levels. There really isn't any particular standard for people out there in the world. I believe that this survey—and many others—confirm that the easy availability of pornography on the Internet has significantly increased the problem of sexual immorality.

There are 4.2 million porn sites on the Web (12 percent of total Web sites), with 2.5 billion daily pornographic e-mails being sent out. Currently, of all the 68 million daily requests made on search engines like Yahoo or Google, more than 25 percent are for porn sites.[4] And thousands of porn movies are being released every year. The number of Americans feeding on pornography is growing at an alarming rate.

Consider this frightening statistic: In 2000, "Envisional, a company in the United Kingdom, reported that it had found nearly 12,000 examples of well-known toy names buried in the metatags of pornography Web sites, 30 percent of which were hard-core."[5] Many pornographers are believed to be using well-known brand names such as Barbie, Disney, Nintendo, and NBA as key words in metatags to attract hits from search engines. For instance, for our Web site, www.pastorjoe.com, I can pay any of the search engines to make sure that every time somebody keys in the word *Bible* as a search topic, my Web site comes up in the top ten. Many porn sites are doing the same— they pay to have metatags with key words such as *NBA* or *Barbie* in the top listing of search engines. So your young daughter may be looking on the Web to check out Barbie dolls, and with just one click of the mouse, be inundated with porn sites. Sexual bombardment is coming after us—and our children and youth—in all kinds of dishonest ways.

Following are some alarming facts from a story that aired on a televised documentary in 2003. Sadly, these figures have only increased. The documentary's narrator reported that in the space of only a generation, a product that once was only available in the back alleys of big cities is now delivered directly into homes and hotel rooms by some of the biggest companies in the United States.

It is estimated that Americans spend more money on adult entertainment than they spend attending professional sporting events, buying music, or going out to the movies. Consumer demand is so strong that some of America's biggest brand names are involved in it. Traditional news magazines and satellite television networks sell more graphic sex films than *Hustler* and *Playboy*. Most of the big hotel chains offer adult films on in-room pay-per-view television systems. According to a source who didn't wish to be identified, nearly half of all the major hotel guests purchase pornography in their rooms, accounting for a huge percent of their in-room profits. One hotel owner said their guests demand it so they have to provide it or lose them as customers.

The documentary reported that the pornography business currently has all the characteristics of a legitimate industry and enjoys considerable economic clout. They have their own conventions and trade publications and host marketing and legal seminars throughout the country. The porn industry even has its own lobbyist in Washington, DC! It is a very large industry in California alone, employing thousands of people and paying millions of dollars in tax revenue.

Pornography and the Law

And what about the laws of this nation? What is federal law on pornography? The only explicit, hardcore sexual material that is absolutely illegal by law in the U.S. today is child pornography—all other material must be put before a jury. The Supreme Court last defined obscenity as material appealing to a degrading interest in sex, depicting it in a patently offensive manner, and lacking any serious artistic, literary, or scientific value. But this was way back in 1973, before the VCR, [DVD] and the Internet were in existence.

I'm not on a witch hunt, and I'm not trying to attack any company or any individual. I'm not going to boycott cable or satellite television or picket hotels, and I am not advising that you should do that either. I'm just trying to paint a true picture of today's world—a world that is pulling out all the stops to try to grab us and drag us into a life of sexual sin and pornography. It is happening all around us every day.

> Many are caught in a web of deceit that tries to convince them that since they are not physically involved with or hurting another person, sex is okay.

So do you think fantasizing in any way, including through the use of pornography, is wrong? Or do you think it is okay? We've discovered there is plenty available! Many are caught in a web of deceit that tries to convince them that since they are not *physically* involved with or hurting another person, sex is okay. Allow me to do my best to bring out God's opinion on this subject.

Matthew 5 relates the account of Jesus giving the Sermon on the Mount. As thousands of people listened, He began speaking about the Law of Moses, which includes a lot of commandments. After telling the crowd, "You shall not murder," and adding explanation on that subject (see verses 21-22 NKJV), He gets to the subject of adultery. People of that day knew that the commandment said, "Thou shalt not commit adultery." (See v. 27 and Exodus 20:14). And they knew that it was wrong to have sex with someone other than their wife. This was very clearly taught in the Law of Moses, part of the Jewish Bible which is now part of the Christian's Old Testament.

But then Jesus said something that was absolutely fascinating:

> *"You have heard that it was said to those of old, 'You shall not commit adultery.' But I say to you that whoever **looks at a woman to lust** for her **has already committed adultery with her in his heart."***
> —Matthew 5:27-28 NKJV (emphasis mine)

That is a powerful statement, and I'm sure it got the attention of the crowd. In His own way, Jesus was saying, "You can boast that you've never actually had sex with a woman other than your wife, but if you are lusting in your heart, it is the same as committing adultery." The same goes for women lusting after other men.

Jesus opened up the issue of sexual sin and clearly explained that fantasizing sexual acts is just as bad to God as the actual act. If you are married and you fantasize about sex with someone other than your mate—which usually happens when you're involved in pornography—God says it is the same as actually having an affair. Now, I realize that an affair would have greater outward consequences because there's actual physical activity, but in the eyes of God, both are considered adultery.

I know we spoke to the issue of sex and singles in the last chapter, but I must reiterate something here. If you're single and you get involved in pornography, fantasizing, masturbation, and all of those things, in God's eyes it is sin. Let's take a moment to address the issue of masturbation. Some Christian leaders and many psychologists teach that masturbation is normal and not a sin. They firmly believe it's necessary for proper sexual development. I think you've figured out by now that I'm not an intellectual genius, nor a psychologist. I do, however, understand the Bible somewhat. I may be missing something here, but before I was saved, while I was single, I could never masturbate without thinking about some type of sexual scenario.

God's plan is for us to be sexually pure.

If someone could masturbate with a blank mind, maybe it wouldn't be wrong. But I don't think that's possible, at least from my frame of reference. Because of this simple truth and the Matthew 5 scripture just referenced, I have to say—and have taught my own children—that masturbation is not a godly thing to do. Some married couples have asked me if it's okay to masturbate while thinking about their mate. Talk about being uncomfortable with a question! My words to them were, "If your mate is okay with it, I guess that's the one person you can fantasize about. However, why? Why not do the real thing with them? Why do it on your own?" You may be thinking about now that I think too hard! For sure, we know God's plan is for us to be sexually pure, and that's why He wants us to know that sexual sin begins in the heart and mind. And that is just as bad as committing sexual sin physically. I realize that Jesus does not say it's a sin to see a man or a woman and notice that they're attractive. That's not a sin. But He does tell us that if we begin to fantasize about sexual acts and lust after a man or woman in that way, we've committed sin.

Sexual sin was also a topic in the Old Testament.

*"If I've let myself **be seduced by a woman** and **conspired to go to bed with her**, fine, my wife has every right to go ahead and sleep*

*with anyone she wants to. **For disgusting behavior like that,** I'd deserve the worst punishment you could hand out. Adultery is a fire that burns the house down; I wouldn't expect anything I count dear to survive it."*
—Job 31:9-12 THE MESSAGE
(emphasis mine)

Job is examining his heart, and he says, "I've been faithful to my wife. I have been a good husband. I haven't slept around." Then he points out that lust is shameful—a crime—a sin so bad that it should be punished. God has consistently taught mankind that sex is for marriage only and outside of marriage it's wrong—even Job knew that!

Earlier in this book, I mentioned how hooked on sex I was before I met Jesus. I'm telling you these things about myself because I want you to know that I'm a guy who grew up in the world just like you probably did. And when I didn't know God, I practiced all types of sexual sin and other sins. My heart is not to condemn anyone, but to convince you of God's opinion on these hot sex issues. Allow me to further prove that sexual fantasizing and pornography are wrong in God's eyes. The Bible provides some interesting information about how important it is to guard our hearts and minds. These are the words of Jesus:

> *"It is **the thought-life that defiles you.**
> For from within, out **of a person's heart,**
> come evil thoughts, **sexual immorality,**
> theft, murder, adultery, greed, wickedness,
> deceit, eagerness for **lustful pleasure**, envy,
> slander, pride, and foolishness. All these vile
> things **come from within**; they are what
> defile you and make you unacceptable to
> God."*
>
> —Mark 7:20-23 NLT (emphasis mine)

In these four verses, Jesus clearly declares that sin originates in the mind. The outward act is simply a manifestation of what we're thinking and what's inside of us. I think the above verse, and others we've looked at, prove that sin is sin on the inside the same as it is on the outside. I believe these verses are letting us know that sexual fantasizing and pornography are just as bad as the actual act in the eyes of God. Remember, my heart is not to condemn you. If this is God's opinion, then all Christians can and should live up to it! And we can!

God's Opinion in Review
Chapter 4

▎ So much pornography is available today that the American public can hardly avoid it. Even seemingly reputable, traditional news magazine companies, cable and satellite television networks, and many of the major hotel chains whose names you would know and recognize offer and profit from the distribution of pornography.

▎ The only explicit, hard-core sexual material that is absolutely illegal in the U.S. is child pornography—all other material must be put before a jury. The Supreme Court last defined obscenity as material appealing to a degrading interest in sex, depicting it in a patently offensive manner, and lacking any serious artistic, literary, or scientific value.

▎ Jesus opened up the issue of sexual sin in the book of Matthew and clearly explained that fantasizing about sexual acts is just as bad to God as the actual act.

▎ God sees such things as fantasizing and masturbation as sin. Despite the fact that some Christian leaders and many psychologists teach that masturbation is not a sin, from my perspective—you can't masturbate without thinking (fantasizing) about some type of sexual scenario. God's plan is for us to be sexually pure.

■ Even in the Old Testament book of Job, there is teaching about the importance of husbands and wives being faithful to each other and their marriage commitment.

■ Jesus declares that sex originates in the mind in Mark 7:20-23. The outward act is simply a manifestation of what we're thinking and what's inside of us. It is God's opinion that sexual fantasizing and viewing pornography are not acceptable behavior.

Sex with Others, When You're Married?

AND THEY LIVED HAPPILY ever after!" The majority of young girls grow up dreaming of the prince charming that is going to come and knock them off their feet with perfect love and undying loyalty. They dream of marrying a man who is going to love them forever and desires only them for the rest of their days—a man who awakens each morning with accolades and praises toward them. Conversely, most men grow up thinking they're going to marry the perfect sex partner who wants to bless them with pleasure over and over again, all in the same day. One day better and more active then the next! They dream of a wife who will be focused solely on their needs, feeding them grapes while fanning them with loving eyes that are captivated by their masculinity.

In so many cases, after being married for a few months, the best they can do is hope that they make it through another day without killing each other! The marriage fantasy bubble is broken at that point and they realize that people are people—even their mates.

I think most couples go into a marriage with the ideal, "till death do us part!" But then real life begins and for most married couples, month after month, year after year, they find themselves sinking into a mediocre relationship that sometimes is barely even a friendship. Or life wears them out as they raise kids, work, keep up the house, and struggle through the many tests and disappointments that come along. At this point the joy and excitement of marriage is lost in the everyday cares of life. This so often opens the door to a "grass is greener over there" mentality. This can lead people, good people, to the deception that having a relationship with another person who really understands them (this almost

If we follow God's instructions for marriage, we will overcome all frustrations and actually have a marriage that is fun and full of excitement in every area.

inevitably leads to a sexual relationship) would make everything better!

If we follow God's instructions for marriage, we will overcome all frustrations and actually have a marriage that is fun and full of excitement in every area. It's amazing that God's instruction to husbands and wives lets us know that we have to place a positive force into motion in order to overcome our natural self-centered tendencies. I've had a great marriage which began in 1983! Yet Gina and I have walked through many an argument and experienced years of bickering over the same thing, wondering if we would ever solve the problem. What has kept us together and made each year better than the one before and made 95 percent of all our days together fun and worthwhile is operating in God's principles for marriage. That's right, we've had a few bad days!

I'd have to lie to say every day of my marriage has been perfect bliss. We've had a few days that seemed to come from hell itself. Possibly they could be interpreted as someone's idea of hell. One of our most memorable fights took place about seven years into our marriage. We had two children at the time and lived in a tiny 1,100-square-foot house.

This day found us arguing over a certain area of our relationship that we hadn't fixed in seven years! It was heated, and I walked out of the room and went downstairs to pace and vent. About a half hour later I went back upstairs to deal with the problem and talk it out and found Gina sleeping in the bedroom. In her defense, it was one o'clock in morning. Being the spiritual giant that I was at the time, I was so angry that I set the alarm clock for one minute into the future. I then made the alarm ring as loud as possible. I must say, that was the most annoying alarm we ever owned! I then held the clock an inch above Gina's ear and waited the few seconds it took for it to go off. I had a scowl on my face that would have made the devil nervous!

The alarm rang and Gina jumped up in a state of panic. When she looked at me, she freaked out. I told her, "We aren't done yet!" I must remind you that I was the pastor of a large and growing church at the time. All of those people looked to me for spiritual guidance, and here I was startling my wife out of a sound sleep to finish an argument that was seven years in the running and not yet solved! Of course, now I'm fully mature and act just like Jesus would every day of my life. And by the way, Santa Claus is real, and the Easter Bunny is my cousin.

If a person like me, who really loves God and serves Jesus with everything I have, struggles with having a perfect marriage, what is happening to so many other well-meaning people? If you were to ask Gina if I'm a great husband, she would say yes, at least when I'm narrating her answer. No, she'd say yes because I have practiced the marriage principles, as has she, and they have helped us to walk through every circumstance and come out on the other side loving each other even more.

I think it would be very valuable to share these marriage principles with you at this time. I really think our world—with the help of the devil and his helpers, who tempt us with thoughts to do wrong—destroy many a good marriage which began with two loving people who are pure in heart. Most couples start their marriage with the thought in mind, "Till death do us part!"

Let's talk about these marriage-strengthening principles. The Bible places the bulk of the responsibility for the success of a marriage on the man. He must put the number one and most important principle into motion.

> *Husbands, love your wives, __just as__*
> *__Christh__ loved the church and gave himself up*
> *for her....*
> —Ephesians 5:25 NIV (emphasis mine)

If a marriage is going to be successful and the husband and wife are to stay faithful to one another and stay together, this principle must be enacted daily by the husband. How does it look for a husband to love his wife in the same way that Jesus loved the church? There are three key characteristics that the husband must walk in if he's going to love his wife in the same way Christ loved us. Take a look at how Jesus loved us.

1: Jesus initiated love in His relationship with us.

> *We love Him because He first loved us.*
>
> —1 John 4:19 NKJV

2: Jesus loved us where we were in life at the time.

> *But because of his great love for us, God, who is rich in mercy, made us alive with Christ even when we were dead in transgressions—it is by grace you have been saved.*
>
> —Ephesians 2:4, NIV

3: Jesus laid down his life for us. He died so we can live!

> *This is how we know what love is: Jesus Christ laid down his life for us....*
>
> —1 John 3:16, NIV

Wow! Jesus is a tough act to follow! Let me make it very clear—this type of loving doesn't come naturally from me or 99.9 percent of other men. We have to *purpose* to love this way, and it's a daily adjustment to our natural mentality. How do we take these three characteristics of Christ's love and daily place them into motion in our marital unions? First, we must love first. That means that we're not waiting around to see what our wives are going to do for us, but we're constantly the initiator of love in our marriage. This means the husband isn't given the liberty to keep score. Husbands must mentally start every day with the score at zero to zero and understand that God wants us to score first that day! God created the woman to respond and the man to initiate. There is love waiting to pour out of a wife who will respond as the husband initiates love in the relationship.

> The husband must accept his wife for who she is and what she is and not love her on conditions of her changing.

This is what I did with Jesus. When I found out that He loved me first and what He did for me through His death, burial, and resurrection, I gave Him my undying loyalty and life. Wives will do the same thing when they know that they are loved unconditionally!

The next characteristic is very powerful. The husband must accept his wife for who she is and what she is and not love her on conditions of her changing. Now, I realize there are exceptions to this rule. For instance, if a wife is sleeping around or has a substance abuse, a husband would have to confront her and draw a boundary that would place her in a position to have to change. Certain things need an intervention! But I'm referring to the normal, everyday things.

A husband should accept his wife for what and who she is and love her at that place in life. It's not good for a husband to always find fault with his wife, point it out, and demand that she change. He needs to just love her unconditionally and allow God to change her, like He changes all of us! When I discovered that Jesus loved me when I was in a state of sin, my heart was endeared to Him. This knowledge made me love Him all the more. It also made me want to change and become everything that pleased Him! Wives will respond with a similar attitude.

The final characteristic of God's love toward us is the lay-down-your-life attitude! Husbands don't have to die physically for their wives as Jesus died for the church, but God does want us to have a lay-down-your-life attitude. I think it's more difficult to lay down your life daily, putting your wife's needs before your own, than to die physically!

I know my natural, daily tendency is to put Joe's needs first and everyone else's needs behind mine! Gina who? The results are remarkable when we husbands will lay down our lives for our wives. When they see us putting their needs first, they will want to bless us in return. Marriage should be a blessed circle instead of a vicious cycle! The man is the one responsible for bringing this to pass. I didn't know this when I was first married. Coming to understand it has not made our marriage perfect, but it is a happy one! Think about the change that can happen in a marriage if these principles are initiated by the husband. Why would a wife want to leave this? Remember, these things don't come naturally to men. Men must remind themselves of them daily.

God also gives the wife one key instruction. It has been twisted and misinterpreted over the years. I'll do my best to help you understand the heart of God in this instruction.

> *Wives, **submit to your husbands** as to the Lord. For the **husband is the head of the wife** as Christ is the head of the church, his body, of which he is the Savior. Now as the church submits to Christ, so also wives **should submit to their husbands in everything.***
> —Ephesians 5:22-24, NIV (emphasis mine)

If a husband loves his wife as Christ loves the church, most wives would spit shine their shoes and cut their toenails! What does *submission* mean in this context? Does it mean blind obedience? Does it mean that the wife is Cinderella and the husband is one of the evil step sisters, ruling over her? Is it a nicer version of a master and a slave? I remember when I was first married and read these verses from Ephesians. Having grown up in a first-generation Italian family and watching a few of my relatives—not my parents—have their wives walk five feet behind them and serve them like a slave, it was easy to interpret the Bible through tainted glasses.

> If a husband loves his wife as Christ loves the church, most wives would spit shine their shoes and cut their toenails!

My idea of a wife was a woman who waited on me hand and foot and existed solely to please and serve me. I was a good Christian, the pastor of a church, and I really loved my wife. I was also a good person, but I somehow felt that my wife was somewhat a piece of property that God had blessed me with. Over time I realized that I was not correct!

On top of this wrong perception, it is inbred in a man to dominate a woman. This is part of the curse of sin that came when Adam and Eve sinned. At the conclusion of Genesis 3:16, God said the man would rule over the woman. The word *rule* means to be over and control like a master over a slave. That is, the man would dominate the woman! This isn't what God wants. It is the result of man yielding to his sinful nature. God was simply telling all women that it would happen now that a man was born into a sinful state.

This is why we see such terrible treatment of women in third-world countries. I believe the commandment God gave husbands, "Love your wives as Christ loved the church," is meant to supersede this natural, sinful desire that tries to raise itself up in men. I noticed this terrible sin nature coming out of my own sons when they were about five years old and up. They tried to dominate their mom. They didn't want to listen to her and often disrespected her. They treated her much differently than they treated me. I had to discipline and teach this sinful desire out of them. And it worked!

Imagine a man, with his sinful nature and a sinful desire to dominate his wife, reading the verse, "Wives, submit to your husbands!" It's a disaster waiting to happen.

Let's discuss what it means to be the biblical head of the home and to submit. It is important for us to realize that each of the three persons of the godhead, the Father, Son (Jesus), and the Holy Spirit are equal and they are one. God the Father is no more God than Jesus the Son or the Holy Spirit. But there is a head of the godhead—a person who makes the final call—a person who leads. That head is God the Father. (1 Corinthians 11:3.) Jesus is submitted to God the Father in the same way a wife should be submitted to her husband.

Let's ask ourselves some questions about Jesus' relationship with God the Father. Is God the Father better than Him? No, they're equal! Jesus said if you have seen me you've seen the Father; the Father and I are one! (See John 10:30, 14:9-11.) Submission can't be referring to being a lesser, slave-like individual. Jesus isn't a slave to God the Father. They are one, and they are on the same page, having the same goals in life. As a matter of fact, God the Father has given Jesus a place of great authority on the earth and placed everything in heaven, on earth, and below the earth under Him. (Ephesians 1:20-23.) Understanding this relationship provides safety guidelines that keep us from going into the ditch of bad Bible interpretation.

The words *submit* and *submission* originate from a Greek word that means to be under authority, thus the head. I believe that in the context of marriage, it simply means that the wife looks to the husband as the one with vision and direction for the family—the one who is the spiritual leader of the family. I think it best translates like this: "To be desirous to please and be willing to mold." Someone has to take the lead in any relationship or there will be chaos. On the other hand, if the husband loves his wife as Christ loved the church, he doesn't want to do anything without putting her first and finding out what her desires are so he can lay down his life for her. Are you getting the point? It's a blessed circle!

I don't have to tell my wife to submit. I really want to know what she thinks because my goal is to please her and lay my life down for her. She, on the other hand, is always respectful to ask me what I think and to listen to my heart. Because I'm not perfect like God the Father, I also need her to let me know when she disagrees with a direction I want to go. Come on, we're not perfect men, and we need balance in our lives. Enough of this, "I'm the head stuff." Listen to me. Yes, men are to be the lead person, but the husband's heart should be to lay it all down for his wife!

Wives, don't try to control your husbands, because they'll resent it and close down. Have a biblically submissive attitude and show them great respect.

> *However, each one of you also must love his wife as he loves himself, and **the wife must respect her husband.***
> —Ephesians 5:33 NIV (emphasis mine)

Working these principles has made our marriage great and has helped me get back on track when my sinful nature has gotten the best of me. My heart breaks for the couple that doesn't understand these things. I believe that this, along with people not knowing how to conquer sin (later chapter of this book), is a major reason we see so many divorces and such a high level of unfaithfulness in marriages.

Let's find out God's opinion on us staying with one mate and working it out whenever possible. If you have gone through a divorce, whether you were to blame or not, there is always forgiveness. If you're on the edge of divorce or you've been thinking about having an affair, I trust this chapter will help you put every possible effort into trying to save your marriage. I do realize that it takes two for a marriage to work and sometimes one just won't cooperate and divorce happens.

Let's examine what God thinks about marital faithfulness by looking at three very pointed and clear sections of His Word.

> ***Marriage should be honored*** *by all, and* ***the marriage bed kept pure,*** *for God will* ***judge the adulterer*** *and all the* ***sexually immoral.*** *... Be content with what you have, because God has said, "Never will I leave you; never will I forsake you." So we say with confidence, "The Lord is my helper; I will not be afraid. What can man do to me?"*
>
> —Hebrews 13:4-6 (emphasis mine)

*"**You shall not commit adultery**."*

—Exodus 20:14 (emphasis mine)

The LORD *said to Moses, "Speak to the Israelites and say to them: 'I am the* LORD *your God. You must not do as they do in Egypt, where you used to live, and you must not do as they do in the land of Canaan, where I am bringing you. Do not follow their practices. You must obey my laws and be careful to follow my decrees. I am the* LORD *your God. Keep my decrees and laws, for the man who obeys them will live by them. I am the* LORD*.*

*"'**Do not have sexual relations with your neighbor's wife** and defile yourself with her.*

*"'**Everyone who does any of these detestable things**—such persons must be cut off from their people. Keep my requirements and do not follow any of the detestable customs that were practiced before you came and do not defile yourselves with them. I am the* LORD *your God.'"*

—Leviticus 18:1-5, 20, 29-30

(emphasis mine)

I don't think anyone can argue about what God's opinion is with regard to a married person having sex with someone other than their spouse. He truly did create us to become one flesh and to be sexually active only with the one we marry! If you're struggling with the desire to have an affair, fight it and begin to place the marriage principles into motion. If you are currently involved in an affair, God wants you to walk away and begin to restore your marriage to a place of fulfillment and fun!

Let's paint a picture of the American landscape. You'll notice that most of mainstream America isn't aware of God's opinion on this subject. I share these things because all of us are being bombarded by them. I found these statistics to be very interesting. "A recent George Barna poll found that 36 percent of self-proclaimed born-again Christians approve of cohabitation, and 39 percent said indulging in sexual fantasies is morally acceptable—despite biblical principles to the contrary. Peter Brandt, Focus on the Family's issues response director, said, 'To a great extent, the church has lost its moral moorings on sexual behavior.'"[1]

> "To a great extent, the church has lost its moral moorings on sexual behavior."

I hope to change this statistic, at least in your life! Let's look further at the state of America when it comes to marital unfaithfulness.

"The 2000 census offered dramatic evidence of what many have witnessed in their own families and neighborhoods: Many Americans no longer see marriage as the necessity it once was. Not for financial security. Not for sexual intimacy. Not even for raising children. A Gallup poll [in 2001] found 60 percent of Americans no longer think sex outside marriage is wrong."[2] What a bleak picture of the lack of moral standards in America this is. As a pastor, my job is not to condemn people who are not Christians. My job is to put God's moral standard out there and say, "In Christ, there's a better way. He has a way that will keep you from getting in trouble and feeling severe pain." I think we can agree that we have a problem when 60 percent of Americans no longer think sex outside marriage is wrong.

"Adultery is one of the most terrible 'facts of life' in contemporary America," according to Nathan Tabor in the *Canada Free Press* in September 2005.

> If you watch the daily soap operas on TV—many of which are just soft-core pornography—you might come away with the impression that there are more people cheating on their spouses than those who

are remaining faithful. And you might be right. How many people have affairs? That's hard to say because not everybody will answer honestly. But sex therapist Peggy Vaughan, author of *The Monogamy Myth*, conservatively estimates that about 60 percent of married men and 40 percent of married women will have an affair at some time during their marriage. Since [this] book was written more than a decade ago and since more women are leaving the home and entering the workforce, the number of wives having affairs may also have reached the 60 percent range.

Americans have a schizophrenic attitude toward adultery. While 90 percent admit that adultery is morally wrong, according to a *Time-CNN* poll, 50 percent say that [former] President Bill Clinton's morals are "about the same as the average married man." While 35 percent think that adultery should be a crime, 61 percent think it shouldn't.

Why do husbands and wives cheat on their spouses? Psychologists cite subjective issues like loss of love and feelings of alienation. Certainly the media pressure of our sex-saturated society is a significant influence. But a major factor is the easy availability of cheap and plentiful Internet pornography.

Statistics show that 25 percent of all Internet search engine requests are related to pornography. According to the National Coalition for the Protection of Children and Families, "approximately 40 million people in the United States are sexually involved with the Internet." And while 76 percent of women feel that phone sex or cyber-sex is the equivalent of committing adultery, only 41 percent of men do.[3]

The article concludes, "The act of adultery is childish and selfish, and it hurts everyone involved. It violates at least two of the Ten Commandments: the clear prohibitions against committing adultery and coveting your neighbor's spouse. If we care about the future of our great nation, we as a people must relearn the virtue and necessity of staying committed to the spouses to whom we are married."[4]

Mr. Tabor is right. We must "relearn the virtue and necessity of staying committed" to the spouses we married. In addition to these "alarming" findings, there were some "surprising" results of my searches, such as the fact that there are actually "How-to" books about having an affair!

If you are one who has been thinking that the grass might be greener on the other side of the fence, I want to tell you that the grass is not greener over there. And if you cross the line looking for greener grass, you're going to hurt yourself, in one way or another, as well as others and possibly even destroy your life. Yes, God can fix it, but you're going to suffer some unbelievable pain on the way, and it won't be God's fault...nor will it be His judgment. Breaking God's principles and laws will result in pain and trouble.

> Breaking God's principles and laws will result in pain and trouble.

If I were to jump from a five-story building, it is certain that I would get hurt. The impact might break all the bones in my body and even kill me. But could anyone say that God did that? No. If I defy the law of gravity, I'm going to get hurt. So it is with breaking God's law as recorded in the Bible. If we defy His law, it will negatively affect our lives in many ways—and perhaps the lives of many others. Sure, God can repair the damage, but how much better it is to be wise enough to follow God's law and enjoy His blessings.

Many believe there is no pain involved in marital unfaithfulness and they encourage people to participate in it. For example, in 1999, Universal Publishers published author H. Cameron Barnes' 221-page book called *Affair! How to Manage Every Aspect of Your Extramarital Relationship with Passion, Discretion, and Dignity.* Now, you may have "passion," but in this scenario, I would call it lust. And "discretion and dignity" are not found in extramarital affairs. The publisher described this book as "a thoughtful, detailed discussion of every aspect of considering, preparing for, beginning, and conducting a successful and emotionally fulfilling extramarital affair. Contrary to what the media likes to portray, many of the major pitfalls are avoidable and an extramarital relationship can bring a person greater happiness and personal growth if properly managed. *Affair!* shows how."[5] Again, I have never heard of an affair that was successful or emotionally fulfilling. In any arena whatsoever—Christian and non-Christian—affairs may not be discovered but they always cause a great deal of hurt, not only for the participants but also for others who care about them.

Judith E. Brandt authored a 176-page book in 2002 called *The 50-Mile Rule—Your Guide to Infidelity and Extramarital Etiquette.* This book, according to the publisher's comments on Barnes & Noble's Web site, will show you "how to safely stray." You will "discover who makes a suitable affair partner, the rules you must never break, when to call it quits, and what to do if you're caught. With sensible facts that will help you make smarter decisions when pursuing sex outside of marriage (including the rule that spouse and lover should never live within 50 miles of each other)."[6]

An interview with the *Chicago Tribune* included this interchange with Ms. Brandt—Question: "You say [in your book], 'Don't feel guilty'? That doesn't seem realistic." Answer: "Guilt is basically something built into society to keep you in line. If you're going about your business in a discreet way and you are continuing to take care of your wife and most importantly, your children, there's no reason to feel guilt."[7]

This represents some of what is being said to people in the world today, and I believe you will agree that it is contrary to what the Word of God says. Not only that—it is also contrary to polls and surveys of people who have had affairs. There's no way to have a successful affair. It will be a painful experience every single time. Your mate may not realize why they're hurting but they will hurt.

MSNBC's health editor, Jane Weaver, writes: "For most people in relationships, a commitment means no playing around, ever. That doesn't mean there aren't plenty of love rats out there. About one in five adults in monogamous relationships, or 22 percent, have cheated on their current partner. The rate is even higher among married men. And nearly half of people admit to being unfaithful at some point in their lives, according to the results of the survey by MSNBC.com/iVillage Lust, Love & Loyalty."

This study is significant because more than 70,000 adults completed the online reader survey in February 2007. They answered around 30 questions that revealed their intimate feelings about adultery and what makes them stray or stay faithful.

> Spending years together, exchanging wedding rings, even having children doesn't inoculate a couple against cheating.

"About three-quarters of the survey takers say they've made a monogamous commitment, with a majority either married or remarried. But a significant portion found it easier to make that promise than keep it. Spending years together, exchanging wedding rings, even having children doesn't inoculate a couple against cheating. In fact, married folks with kids—including women with very young children—are nearly as likely to commit adultery as childless couples. The bright side is, while many of us are tempted by the fruit of another, it seems we fear cheating more than we need," the report states.

"Survey takers guessed that twice as many people are having extramarital affairs as really are, estimating that 44 percent of married men and 36 percent of married women are unfaithful. The reality is it's not as rampant as some think, with 28 percent of married men and 18 percent of married women admitting to having a sexual liaison," the survey found.

Tom W. Smith, director of the General Social Survey for the National Opinion Research Center at the University of Chicago conducted the highly respected study, "American Sexual Behavior," a poll of 10,000 people over two decades. The study found that 22 percent of married men and 15 percent of married women have cheated at least once—similar to the results from the MSNBC.com/iVillage survey.

Interestingly, "six in ten cheaters believe they totally got away with their affair and another one in ten felt their partner was suspicious, but never found out for sure. Few cheaters—only 2 percent—were busted in the act. And even when confronted with a partner's suspicions, only 6 percent of both men and women confessed to having an affair."[8]

The Bible teaches us very clearly that we always, in one way or another, pay for sexual sin. The book of Proverbs was written to train young men and women in the wisdom of God, but the wisdom recorded there is good for everyone and relevant to all ages, especially if we didn't know of it when we were young. The words found in Proverbs are meant to train us in such a way that we don't make mistakes that cause us pain. As a pastor, I've counseled many people over the last twenty-plus years, and I can tell you that when people don't follow the wisdom of Proverbs, they experience all the consequences that the book says will happen in their lives. There are natural consequences to sexual sin when you're married and commit adultery.

They'll [Bible teachings] *protect you from wanton women,*
　from the seductive talk of some temptress.
Don't lustfully fantasize on her beauty,
　nor be taken in by her bedroom eyes.
You can buy an hour with a whore for a loaf of bread,
　*but a wanton woman **may well eat you alive.***
Can you *build a fire in your lap*
　and not burn your pants?
Can you *walk barefoot on hot coals*
　and not get blisters?
<u>*It's the same when you have sex with your neigh-bor's wife*</u>*:*
　Touch her and you'll pay for it. *No excuses.*
Hunger is no excuse
　for a thief to steal;
When he's caught he has to pay it back,
　even if he has to put his whole house in hock.
Adultery is a brainless act,
　soul-destroying, self-destructive.
　　　　　—Proverbs 6:24-32 The Message
　　　　　　　(emphasis mine)

Think about this for a minute. If you had a fire in your lap, wouldn't you do everything possible to get rid

You cannot commit adultery without paying a painful price.

of it? And if you tried to walk on hot coals with bare feet, it wouldn't take you very long to get away from the coals. You would quickly experience the pain of your actions. Well, this is a Bible picture that portrays the severity of having an affair once you're married. Build a fire in your lap and not burn your pants? No! Walk barefoot on hot coals and avoid being blistered? Absolutely not! These verses make is abundantly clear that you cannot commit adultery without paying a painful price. Did you catch the last part of this verse? Adultery is a brainless act that destroys the soul and puts a person on a self-destructive path! I don't think there is a quicker and more efficient way to ruin your life than by having an extramarital affair. Here's more of God's opinion:

> *Dear friend, pay close attention to this, my wisdom;*
> > *listen very closely to the way I see it.*
> *Then you'll acquire a taste for good sense;*
> > *what I tell you will keep you out of trouble.*
> <u>*The lips of a* **seductive woman** *are oh so sweet*</u>*,*
> > *her soft words <u>are oh so smooth</u>.*

*But it won't be long before **she's gravel in your mouth,***
*a pain in your gut, **a wound in your heart.***
She's dancing down the primrose path to Death;
*   **she's headed straight for Hell and taking you with her.***
She hasn't a clue about Real Life,
*   about who she is or where she's going.*
                    —Proverbs 5:1-4 THE MESSAGE
                        (emphasis mine)

This scripture presents more proof of what God's opinion is on marital faithfulness! It also alludes to the afterlife. Let's not forget, even if we get away with an affair down here and no one ever finds out, God knows and will hold us accountable on Judgment Day. Whether it's down here or up in heaven, marital unfaithfulness will cost us! Look at these statistics.

According to Dr. Lana Staneli, author of a book on marital triangles, "Of those who break up their marriage to marry someone else [the one they were having the affair with], 80 percent are sorry later." That is huge. And of those who have an affair and get a divorce, only 10 percent marry their lover. Of those who marry the person they had the affair with, 70 percent—that's 70 percent of the 10 percent—get a divorce. This means that only 3 percent of all the people who married their lovers stay married. Of the 25 or 30 percent that stay married—that's 25 or 30 percent of the 10 percent—only half of them are happy. So of 1.5 percent of the people who married their lovers, only 1.5 percent of them are happy.[9] Now, those statistics alone should convince you that the grass is not greener on the other side and extramarital affairs and divorce hurt us and others.

God does give instructions that are true! If you divorce your mate because you are having an affair, both of you will experience great pain. And if, after your affair is exposed, you and your mate decide to stay together, there will be years of walking through almost inconceivable pain as you try to rebuild trust. If you give your life to God and seek Him with all your heart, He will get in there and help you work it out. If you release the marriage principles we spoke of earlier, they will expedite this healing process. But you will still have a difficult time because trust is everything in a relationship, and it takes time to rebuild it.

> Trust is everything in a relationship, and it takes time to rebuild it.

I think you'll agree that we love our children more than anything on the planet. Divorce and infidelity really hurt them. The statistics from divorce are heartbreaking. According to the Heritage Foundation, "Each year, over 1 million American children suffer the divorce of their parents; moreover, half of the children born this year to parents who are married will see their parents divorce before they turn 18. Mounting evidence in social science journals demonstrates that the devastating physical, emotional, and financial effects that divorce is having on these children will last well into adulthood and affect future generations."[10] This effect is seen when these children grow up and get married. "Marriages of the children of divorce actually have a much higher rate of divorce than the marriages of children from intact families. A major reason for this, according to a recent study, is that children learn about marital commitment or permanence by observing their parents. In the children of divorce, the sense of commitment to a lifelong marriage has been undermined."[11] In surveys conducted by the National Opinion Research Center, researchers found that white female children of divorce were 60 percent more likely to undergo divorce or separation in adulthood than a similar population from intact families. The divorce/separation rate for white male children of divorce was 35 percent higher than for white male children from intact families.[12] I have witnessed countless children being hurt through divorce—child after child turning away from God and entering into destructive lifestyles because of divorce. Some are scarred so heavily that it takes far into their adulthood before they overcome its destructive effects—and some never recover.

And beyond this is the financial issue. Many children suffer from the economic hardship created by divorce. "Families with children that were not poor before the divorce see their income drop as much as 50 percent. Almost 50 percent of the parents with children that are going through a divorce move into poverty after the divorce."[13] And beyond the cost to the family, society must pay a price as well. "Marriages that end in divorce also are very costly to the public. One researcher determined that a single divorce costs state and federal governments about $30,000, based on such things as the higher use of food stamps and public housing as well as increased bankruptcies and juvenile delinquency. The nation's 1.4 million divorces in 2002 are estimated to have cost the taxpayers more than $30 billion."[15]

We truly have a problem of sexual immorality in America. It has caused many divorces but isn't the sole cause. And I believe God wants the church to be an example to the world. An example in the area of purity but also great marriages that have no open doors! Married people who are in extramarital affairs need to understand that they are missing out on an incredible blessing that only comes with sex within the marital relationship! Work on the other issues that are out of order in your marriage and place God's principles into motion. You will soon see remarkable changes!

God's Opinion in Review
Chapter 5

▌ The majority of women grow up believing Prince Charming is coming to sweep them off their feet, he'll love them forever, and make everything in life perfect. Most men dream of marrying the perfect sex partner who desires to bless them with pleasure on cue (just like the movies). Then real life sets in. The fantasy bubble breaks and the realization comes that people are just people, with many faults and imperfections.

▌ Life sometimes wears out married couples as they raise children, work, maintain a home, and struggle through the many tests and disappointments that inevitably come with life. It doesn't take that much for the grass to look greener on the other side of the fence.

▌ Satan and his helpers work overtime to place temptation in our paths. Temptation to cheat on our spouse destroys many marriages that began with two loving people whose hearts were pure.

- Successful marriages are the result of husbands loving their wives in the same way that Jesus loved the church. There are three characteristics that the husband must walk in if he's going to love his wife this way: (1) Jesus initiated love in His relationship with us as written in 1 John 4:19; (2) Jesus loved us where we were in life at the time, according to Ephesians 2:4; (3) Jesus laid down His life for us. He died so we can live, according to 1 John 3:16. These principles must be enacted daily. It does not come naturally to men, so it's a daily adjustment to their natural mentality.

- Marriage should be a blessed circle instead of a vicious cycle.

- The submission verses in Ephesians 5:22-24 have been twisted and misinterpreted. It does not mean blind obedience, husbands ruling over their wives, or a nicer version of master and slave. It does not mean that women are designed strictly to please and serve their husbands. This is not what God wants!

- The Father, Son, and Holy Spirit are equal and one. They are the example put forth in the New Testament for our contemporary households. God is the head, Jesus is submitted to God the Father in the same way a wife should be submitted to her husband. But God is not better or more important than Jesus. They are equal.

▌ Wives would have no trouble submitting to a husband who is submitted to God, the Father almighty, and puts her first—even to the point of laying down his life for her. Enough of this "I'm the head" stuff! And wives must not try to control their husbands, but show them a submissive attitude and proper respect.

▌ With God, adultery is not an option. He truly did create us to become one flesh and to be sexually active only with the one we marry.

▌ The act of adultery is selfish and childish, and it hurts everyone involved. Though books have been written about how to have an extramarital affair, no one benefits and the statistics prove that when the affair results in divorce and remarriage to that extramarital partner, divorce soon follows. Six in ten cheaters believe they got away with their affair. Only two percent were busted in the act. The Bible clearly teaches that we pay, one way or the other, for sexual sin.

▌ Mounting evidence demonstrates that the devastating physical, emotional, and financial effects that divorce is having on children will last well into adulthood and affect future generations. Research shows that children of divorced parents actually have a much higher rate of divorce than the marriages of children from intact families. Children learn about marital commitment or permanence by observing their parents. In the children of divorce, commitment to a lifelong marriage is undermined.

∎ Beyond the other startling statistics of divorce is the financial issue. Many children suffer from the economic hardship created by divorce. Families that were not poor before the divorce see their income reduced by as much as 50 percent, placing some children at near poverty levels.

∎ Work on the issues that are out of order in your marriage and place God's principles into motion. You will soon see remarkable changes!

Sex with the Same Sex?

OUR WORLD NEEDS TO KNOW God's opinion on the subject of homosexuality more so than ever in our history. I remember growing up when this issue was kept in the closet, so to speak, but now it's lived out loud. We are being pressured into accepting this lifestyle as normal. Remember, I'm not writing this book to force non-Christians to live according to God's opinion. I am writing it to help Christians understand how God wants us to view things and live our lives. What does God have to say about this issue? Is His opinion in line with the current belief of the nation and world where we live? I hope to help you see God's opinion and then you can judge for yourself.

Is sex wrong with someone of the same sex? We will also discuss gay marriage in this chapter. I think it best to begin by learning about what those who came out of this lifestyle through Christ have to say about it.

Joe Dallas is the former president of Exodus International, now known as Exodus Global Alliance, a ministry that in its own words, "equips Christians and churches to uphold the biblical view of sexuality but respond with compassion and grace to those affected by homosexuality, proclaiming that change is possible through the transforming power of Jesus Christ." This is a remarkably extraordinary ministry. I can only say so much about the organization in this chapter, but if you want to know more about becoming free from the homosexual lifestyle or God's perspective from a position of mercy, you can go to www.exodusglobalalliance. org. They provide many sensitive and practical helps on their Web site. They host meetings all over the country that anyone can attend. Joe Dallas says, "*Homophobia is a word that has been cleverly used to paint anyone who objects to homosexuality with the broad brush of bigotry. It's a relatively new word, first coined by psychologist George Wineburg in 1972. It was originally*

> Change is possible through the transforming power of Jesus Christ.

intended to mean 'dread of being in close quarters with homosexuals.' Thirty years later its meaning has broadened considerably. It is now used to apply to any person, expression, or belief that does not place homosexuality on par with heterosexuality. And because it's such a negative term, like racist or sexist, it intimidates many people from sharing God's opinion on this subject. Who, after all, wants to be known as a bigot?"[1]

Mr. Dallas makes a valid point here, and I want to be sure you know that I am not homophobic. I love people and have genuine compassion for those who struggle with homosexuality and other sexual sin. I see no difference between those who are challenged by that specific struggle and anyone who struggles with sin of any kind. This book is definitely not designed to cut down those who contend with homosexuality. I want to help set people free. My heart is to present what God has to say about it and to try to bring the facts to light.

I do not believe that anyone was born a homosexual. Someone can have tendencies in that direction and it can be easier for them to fall into. There is a real devil, and I'm convinced that he wants to deceive us into believing people are born that way. If you believe you're born this way, you won't fight or resist what God calls sin. The devil also is very busy putting sexual thoughts into people's minds and convincing them that they are their own thoughts.

Dr. Stanton Jones, Wheaton College's chief academic officer and second ranking administrator, oversees the graduate and undergraduate programs of Wheaton College and is the author of more than 50 articles and book chapters, including *Modern Psychotherapies: A Comprehensive Christian Appraisal; Homosexuality: The Use of Scientific Research in the Church's Moral Debate;* and the *God's Design For Sex* book series. He teaches counselors how to counsel and minister to people who are trying to come out of the homosexual lifestyle.

I watched some of the videos of this extremely intelligent man, and he cited some old surveys about how many people are homosexual in America. I won't bore you with all the details, but it was amazing to find out some of those old surveys were done in prisons. Can you imagine asking prison inmates if they ever had a homosexual thought? An all-male prison is no place to do this type of survey. It would be slightly skewed, I think. Apparently, however, that's how things were done relative to this subject in the past.

More modern surveys have concluded:

❭ Three percent of males 15-44 years of age have had oral or anal sex with another male in the last 12 months (1.8 million). Four percent of females had a sexual experience with another female in the last 12 months.

❱ The proportion who had same-sex contact in their lifetimes was 6 percent for males and 11 percent for females.

❱ About 1 percent of men and 3 percent of women 15-44 years of age have had both male and female sexual partners in the last 12 months.[2]

These are much lower figures than the media projects to our collective consciousness. Before I researched this subject, I thought perhaps ten percent or more of the American male and female population were actively engaged in the homosexual lifestyle. My explorations continually brought home to me the fact that God loves every single one of us so much that He's willing to point out where we're going astray and point toward the direction in which we should be going.

Personally, I never struggled with homosexuality, but I did struggle with sexual sin as a young man. Through a process of growth in Jesus Christ, He delivered me from sexual sin, and He has delivered hundreds of thousands of others who found themselves in bondage to it—whether it involved same sex or opposite sex issues. He can deliver anyone who is struggling with any type of sin. But he can't deliver us until we accept Christ as our personal Savior and acknowledge that sin is sin.

God has quite a bit to say, however, about the issue of homosexuality. His opinion is found in the Bible, and among the most powerful opinions/arguments about the subject is found in Leviticus 18:20-22. It's simple and straight to the point:

> *"Do not have sexual relations with your neighbor's wife and defile yourself with her. Do not give any of your children to be sacrificed to Molech, for you must not profane the name of your God. I am the LORD.* **Do not lie with a man as one lies with a woman; that is detestable."**

The New King James Version uses the word *abomination* instead of the word *detestable* at the end of the verse. Webster's dictionary says an *abomination* is "extreme dislike or abhorrence; something that elicits extreme dislike."[3] *Detestable* is defined as "deserving abhorrence." And to *detest* something means "to curse; to dislike intensely; abhor."[4] In other words, this is something that's not sweet in the nostrils of God. Now it's also important to point out that the Bible also uses the term, *abomination,* to describe how God feels about somebody who causes division or trouble between Christians. And there are many other issues that God's Word says are an abomination to God. Sometimes we think that God is just coming against the homosexual lifestyle when He uses a word as strong as *abominable* or calls homosexuality an *abomination*, but look at the Leviticus text. There's a list:

❱ Adultery
❱ Child sacrifice
❱ Profaning the name of God
❱ Lying with a man as one lies with a woman (homosexuality)

The Bible sets some clear standards with this list and lets us know, without question, that these lifestyles are wrong and we aren't to touch or be touched by them. Before Jesus, people had difficulty getting free from sin because God wasn't inside of them, but when Jesus and His Holy Spirit came to live inside of us, God was at last in a position to set us free. This freedom comes as we renew our minds, realize what God has to say about sin, and place three principles into motion.

> This freedom comes as we renew our minds, realize what God has to say about sin, and place three principles into motion.

When God tells us something's wrong, He gives us the power and strength through Christ to keep from doing it. He provides the ability to overcome it.

Now, some might say, "Well, Pastor Joe, I hear what you're saying, but that's the Old Testament. God, through Jesus Christ, is a God of love. He doesn't care what we do now. God's not going to punish us for anything now because of Jesus' sacrifice that covered our sin."

Remember, no matter how good we are, if we don't accept Christ, we can't go to heaven. The book of Revelation explicitly describes the judgment of non-Christians:

> *Then I saw a great white throne and him who was seated on it. Earth and sky fled from his presence, and there was no place for them. And I saw the dead, great and small, standing before the throne, and books were opened. Another book was opened, which is the book of life. The dead were judged according to what they had done as recorded in the books. The sea gave up the dead that were in it, and death and Hades gave up the dead that were in them, **and each person was judged according to what he had done.** Then death and Hades were thrown into the lake of fire. The lake of fire is the second death. **If anyone's name was***

*not found written in the book of life, he
was thrown into the lake of fire.*
—Revelation 20:11-15 (emphasis mine)

Anyone who is not in Christ—anyone whose name
is not written in the book of life—will be judged and
thrown into a lake of fire, no matter what sins they've
committed. And those who are in Christ will be judged
concerning the lifestyle we lived and those things for
which we did not repent (2 Corinthians 5:10). All sin
that we willingly committed and didn't repent of will be
judged and dealt with when we Christians stand before
the judgment seat of Christ. This is a very serious issue
to God. He really wants us to live right.

Yes, He is a God of love, but He is also a God who will
have to judge us because He is holy. He has set a holy
standard for us to follow, and it is not just mentioned
in the Old Testament. The apostle Paul wrote a letter to
the church in Rome in A.D. 56 or 57 as he completed
his third missionary journey. The letter is now known
as the book of Romans. Its theme is righteousness. Paul
teaches four important things in this letter:

1. No human being is righteous.
2. Jesus Christ is perfectly righteous.

3. If we have faith in Jesus, we are freed from the power of sin, given a new life, and returned to a right relationship with God.

4. We should live Christian lives that are "holy and pleasing to God."

It's as New Testament as you can get. Then Paul writes about the earth's population prior to the Flood as an example of the lengths God will go to in order to set us straight. He refers to the residents of two cities, Sodom and Gomorrah, and I want you to notice what he has to say concerning these folks:

> *They exchanged the truth of God for a lie, and worshiped and served created things rather than the Creator—who is forever to be praised. Amen. Because of this, God* **gave them over to shameful lusts** [notice what God considers to be shameful lusts]. ***Even their women exchanged natural relations for unnatural ones. In the same way the men also abandoned natural relations with women and were inflamed with lust for one another.*** *Men committed indecent acts with other men, and received in themselves the due penalty for their perversion* [notice how He calls it a perversion].

Furthermore, since they did not think it worthwhile to retain the knowledge of God, he gave them over to a depraved mind, to do what ought not to be done.
—Romans 1:25-28 (emphasis mine)

That's the New Testament, and God is saying that when people take their eyes off the truth, they begin to fall into all kinds of sin. He's telling us this has happened before and God had to send a flood and after that fire to destroy two cities full of sexual sin, homosexuality being the most prevalent. Pastors

> When people take their eyes off the truth, they begin to fall into all kinds of sin.

and church leaders must work hard to keep lifting up God's standards and teaching from the standard of all standards, God's own Word. We have to say, "This is God's opinion about life and how we live it. It's all right here in His Book." Each of us arrives at a place where we have a decision to make: *What am I going to do with Jesus?* Once that decision is made and we're saved, then we have to decide, *Am I going to obey the Bible, God's Word? Am I going to do the right things because God says they're right?*

Jude, like James, was a brother of Jesus. He wrote to warn Christians that God will punish and destroy false teachers who lead people to live sinful lives just as He punished sinners in the Old Testament.

> *In a similar way, Sodom and Gomorrah and the surrounding towns gave themselves up to sexual immorality and perversion. They serve as an example of those who suffer the punishment of eternal fire.*
>
> —Jude 1:7

About Sodom and Gomorrah, Genesis 19:24-25 says, "Then the LORD rained down burning sulfur on Sodom and Gomorrah—from the LORD out of the heavens. Thus he overthrew those cities and the entire plain, including all those living in the cities—and also the vegetation in the land." Look again at the terminology in the New Testament book of Jude that says, "they gave themselves over to sexual immorality and perversion." The word *perversion* as it is used here refers to homosexuality—male or female—and God considers it a sin. He says it is wrong and something that no one should be doing. He wants to deliver people from it.

When you go back to Genesis and read the fascinating account of Sodom and Gomorrah, it speaks of Abraham's nephew, Lot, who lived in Sodom. The gist of the story is that God had decided to destroy Sodom and Gomorrah because of their great and grievous sin, but He shared His plans with Abraham in advance because Abraham was a friend of God. In response to this terrifying news, Abraham pleaded with God to spare his nephew and God complied, sending two angels disguised as men to retrieve Lot and his family before the carnage began. The Bible says the two men found Lot sitting at the gateway to the city with some other men, and Lot invited the two visitors to his home to have dinner and spend the night before they all packed up and left the next morning.

> *Before they had gone to bed, all the men from every part of the city of Sodom—both young and old—surrounded the house. They called to Lot, "Where are the men who came to you tonight? **Bring them out to us so that we can have sex with them.**"*
> —Genesis 19:4-5 (emphasis mine)

It is important to note that *all* the men from *every* part of the city came to Lot's door in search of the two men. Without the Word of God, sin spreads and it spreads far. This is why we must raise God's standard to the world or people will run wild. Can you imagine seeing an angry mob of men surrounding your house and demanding the release of the male guests in your home in order to have sex with them? Obviously, we can agree that homosexuality was rampant in this town.

> *Lot went outside to meet them and shut the door behind him and said, "No, my friends. Don't do this wicked thing. ...Don't do anything to these men, for they have come under the protection of my roof."*
>
> *"Get out of our way," they replied. And they said, "This fellow came here as an alien, and now he wants to play the judge! We'll treat you worse than them." They kept bringing pressure on Lot and moved forward to break down the door. But the men inside reached out and pulled Lot back into the house and shut the door. Then they struck the men who were at the door of the house, young and old, with blindness so that they could not find the door.*
>
> —Genesis 19:6-11

God is so cool! He used the two angels to bring blindness on the angry mob and the problem was gone. Now, my intention is not to condemn anyone, but to paint a picture that homosexuality was so bad during this time that *every* man in an entire city, with the exception of Lot and his family, had fallen under its spell. Wow, I don't think you could say they were all born this way. This lifestyle is as much a sin as any other sin and sin spreads when it's not put in check. In the book of Jude, remember that God called it perversion. The dictionary defines *perversion* as "the act of perverting or state of being perverted," and to be *perverse* means "deviating from what is right or good; obstinately persisting in an error or fault; wrongly self-willed; disposed to contradict and oppose; a sexual practice or act considered deviant."[5] That's something that's not good.

> God remains as opposed to the perverse lifestyle of homosexuality in the New Testament as He did in the Old Testament.

Why do I mention it here? To point out that God remains as opposed to the perverse lifestyle of homosexuality in the New Testament as He did in the Old Testament. The only difference in the New Testament is that God extends His hand of mercy toward all sinners on the condition that the sinner repents and accepts Christ, who will set the sinner free and deliver him/her. God is able to do that for every single person who calls on His name.

Gay Marriage

God's opinion about homosexuality is so clear that we who respect the Bible can correctly conclude that He is also opposed to gay marriage. He loves people and wants to set them free, but these are issues which God is decidedly against. There has been a growing controversy brewing for the past few years about the issue of gay marriage. I collected a bunch of headline news stories over a period of just one month from newspapers that are distributed around the country—papers like the *New York Times, USA Today, The Wall Street Journal, The Chicago Sun Times*—print media anyone has access to via the Internet or on the local newsstand. The stories are buzzing with same sex marriage news, such as:

> ❱ "In an extraordinary act of civil disobedience under the direction of the newly elected mayor, San Francisco begins issuing marriage license to hundreds of same sex couples in defiance of state law."

> ❱ "Having already performed more than 2,900 same sex weddings over the previous week the city of San Francisco takes the state of California to court on the grounds its ban on same sex marriage is unconstitutional."

> ❱ "President Bush announces his support of a constitutional amendment banning same sex marriage saying one is needed to stop judges from changing the definition of the most enduring human institution."

❯ "The mayor of New Platts, NY, is charged with 19 counts of solemnizing a marriage without a license after performing marriage ceremonies for 25 same sex couples."

❯ "California's Supreme Court orders a halt to same sex marriages in the state. Since San Francisco's mayor began issuing licenses a month earlier, more than 3,700 same sex couples have wed, and same sex marriages have taken place in Oregon, New Mexico, New York and New Jersey."

We live in a nation that is being shredded apart by this great controversy, and I believe that people like you and me believe people across America would like to know what God has to say about same sex marriage. From what we've presented so far, I believe there is no doubt that God created men to marry women and women to marry men. That's how we were made. It's God's heart for men and women to cohabitate with one another, make a home, and raise a family. No doubt about it!

I want to close this chapter with one of the most gripping scriptures in the Bible. This scripture is very dear to me. It says:

> *Do you not know that the wicked will*
> *not inherit the kingdom of God? Do not be*
> *deceived: Neither the sexually immoral nor*
> *idolaters nor adulterers nor male prostitutes*
> ***nor homosexual offenders** nor thieves nor*
> *the greedy nor drunkards nor slanderers nor*
> *swindlers will inherit the kingdom of God.*
> —1 Corinthians 6:9-10 (emphasis mine)

What I like about these verses is that everything is mixed in here. It's not just about homosexuals. It is yet another list of most any kind of sin that you can think of, and the answer is still the saving grace of Jesus Christ. Give your heart to Jesus, and He'll set you free and you'll enter into the kingdom of God. Then he makes this statement:

> ***And that is what some of you were.** But*
> *you were washed, you were sanctified, you*
> *were justified in the name of the Lord Jesus*
> *Christ and by the Spirit of our God.*
> —1 Corinthians 6:11 (emphasis mine)

This is why I love this section of scripture. Paul was writing to the church in Corinth, probably in the winter of A.D. 55. He sent this letter while he was in Ephesus in response to a letter from the Corinthian church. In the introduction of 1 Corinthians, the *New International Version* of the Bible states, "The Christians in Corinth . . . were living very sinful lives. Paul wrote this letter to scold them and teach them how Christians should act." There were homosexual offenders—people in the church at Corinth—who had been saved after practicing the homosexual lifestyle and sinning in a multitude of other ways. This fact should bring great hope to all who struggle with this lifestyle.

God wrote to them through Paul, saying, "You know what, guys? You all came out of crazy, sinful backgrounds and this is what some of you *were* (past tense)." Some of the Corinthian Christians who had formerly been homosexuals were now counted among the saints, giving evidence that there is realistic hope for people caught in this lifestyle. He went on to say, "Now you're washed, sanctified, and justified in the name of Jesus." Jesus sets people free from any type of sin they can fall into. And if you are a Christian who has fallen back into that lifestyle of homosexuality or you've just tried it for the first time, I want you to know that God's mercy never ends and His forgiveness never stops. His power is always available to you.

> Jesus sets people free from any type of sin they can fall into.

These are not unpardonable sins, and if you cry out to God and tell Him you truly want to be delivered, God will deliver you and set you free in every area. If you're not a Christian, let me encourage you to give your heart to Jesus and allow Him to do a supernatural work in you just as He did in me. Repent, and He'll forgive you, and He'll restore you to a place of strength and victory in Him.

God's Opinion in Review
Chapter 6

▌ Is sex with the same sex wrong? The Bible, God's opinion, has much to say on the subject, despite the fact that many think there are no direct references to homosexuality in God's Word.

▌ We are being pressured as a society into accepting this lifestyle as normal. *Homophobia* is a word that is cleverly used to paint anyone who objects to homosexuality with the broad brush of bigotry.

▌ Exodus Global Alliance is a ministry that equips Christians and churches to uphold the biblical view of sexuality but respond with compassion and grace to those affected by homosexuality, proclaiming that change is possible through the transforming power of Jesus Christ. Visit **www.exodusglobalalliance. org** for more information.

▌ Although the Bible does not use the word homosexual, Leviticus 18:22 says, "Do not lie with a man as one lies with a woman; that is detestable." The word *detestable* is defined as "deserving abhorrence; to curse; to dislike intensely; abhor." In other words, this is something that is not sweet in the nostrils of God.

- When Jesus and His Holy Spirit came to live on the inside of us, God was in a position to set us free from the bondage of sin. This freedom comes as we renew our minds, realize what God has to say about sin, and place three principles into motion: (1) Understanding what God says is right and what is wrong; (2) Realizing that God gives us the power and strength through Christ to keep from sinning; (3) Accepting God's provision of ability to overcome temptation to sin.

- Anyone who is not in Christ (whose name isn't written in the book of life), will be judged and thrown into a lake of fire, no matter what sins they've committed. And those who are in Christ will be judged concerning the lifestyle they lived and those things for which they did not repent. God is holy. He has to judge us because He is holy. He has set a holy standard for us to follow.

- God's opinion about homosexuality is so clear that we who respect the Bible can correctly conclude that He is also opposed to gay marriage. He loves people and wants to set them free, but these are issues which God is decidedly against.

▮ There is no doubt that God created men to marry women and women to marry men. That's how we were made. It's God's heart for men and women to cohabitate with one another, make a home, and raise a family.

▮ Homosexuality and other sexual sin are not unpardonable sins. You can cry out to God and repent, and He will deliver you in every area of your life. He'll forgive and restore you to a place of strength and victory in Him.

Born Gay?

CHAPTER 7

TODAY'S MAINSTREAM MEDIA works diligently to sell the concept that people are born gay and there's no way for them to avoid living the gay lifestyle. An unsubstantiated study conducted in 1991 by Dr. Simon LeVay continues to be cited in the media suggesting that a tiny section of the brain is larger in heterosexual men than it is in heterosexual women. And that in gay men this part of the brain was the same size as it is in heterosexual women. The study concludes that there is a biological reason for sexual orientation—that people are either born homosexuals or born heterosexuals.[1]

Fortunately, other great minds have shot some really big holes in those conclusions. A more recent study published in the March 2005 issue of the journal, *Human Genetics*, "undermines the commonly held view that homosexual orientation is determined by genetic factors. The study's lead author Brian Mustanski, from the University of Illinois-Chicago said in a UIC news release, 'There is no one gay gene. Sexual orientation is a complex trait, so it's not surprising that we found several DNA regions involved in its expression.' However a thorough examination of the actual report reveals no statistically significant findings for any of these DNA regions. In summary, the Mustanski study finds no significant relationship between DNA regions and self reported sexual orientation. Available evidence suggests that genes may be expressed via the interaction of temperament with certain environments. Practically, then, at present, one cannot know with any degree of certainty that a gene or combination of genes will distinguish why one man is homosexual and another is not."[2]

It is interesting to find a conclusive medical study conducted by a secular physician at a secular university that clearly states the impossibility of determining genetically whether an individual is born a homosexual, because the scientific ability to make that determination is nonexistent. I don't believe anyone is born a homosexual, in the same way people aren't born adulterers, or murderers. The potential to do all these things and more lays dormant in our sin nature, and all of us can cross over to that side. Now, people can have a propensity toward different types of sin, including homosexuality. Remember, 90 percent-plus of the men in Sodom were gay. How can 90 percent of people be born gay? That just doesn't happen in any culture.

I learned so much from an article excerpted from two booklets written by Dr. Joseph Nicolosi called *The Truth Comes Out* and *The Heart of the Matter* on Exodus International's Web site. It discusses the causes of homosexuality, and I'm going to share a lengthy part of the article with you to shed a more focused light on the subject. You can read the entire article and find many other helpful articles at this Web site, http://exodus.to/content/view/504/186/.

> What Causes Homosexuality? Is it a choice? Many Christians will say, "homosexuality is a choice." What do they mean? How does this sound to the ears of someone who's struggling with it? Whether or not to engage in gay sex is entirely a choice, of course, like any sin is a choice. But like other temptations, people do not choose to be tempted with homosexuality. Remember that temptation is not a choice. Rather, it is a given fact of life for all believers (James 1:14-16).

There are many factors that can contribute to a person developing a homosexual orientation. These are some environmental elements that we often see in the backgrounds of people who struggle with homosexuality, and while none of them is present in every struggler's life, most strugglers will identify with one or more:

1. Absent/distant same-sex parent
2. Sexual abuse
3. Bad experience with gender-specific activities (e.g., sports for boys)
4. Name-calling ("fag," "sissy," etc.)
5. Over-involvement with opposite-sex parent
6. Early exposure to pornography or sexual language
7. Isolation from same-sex peers

It is so important to understand that having one or more of these experiences in someone's past will not necessarily make them a homosexual. Lots of young men have had absent or emotionally distant fathers, and while this causes them to have issues, those issues aren't necessarily going to be homosexual in nature. Many young girls who are sexually abused do not develop same-gender attractions, but the vast majority of same-sex attracted women experienced sexual abuse at some point that twisted their understanding of gender and sexuality. What's most crucial is a child's perception of what's going on around them. For instance:

• A boy may have a loving father, but if he misinterprets an event or something his dad says or does, he can perceive that his father does not love him. The boy might respond to the perceived rejection from his father by rejecting his own masculinity.

• People react differently to sexual abuse. It is always bad, but some victims understand that they were victimized, are not at fault, and are able to eventually recover. Others (especially the younger ones) will internalize the experience, asking "What is it about me that made him pick me?" This makes the abuse much more devastating, because it alters their sense of identity: 'He picked me because somehow he knew I was gay.'

The experiences mentioned here create identity confusion that, continuing into puberty, can affect sexuality. It is especially dire when bad experiences combine with a lack of needs being met.[3]

Dr. Nicolosi goes on to say,

I remember a time when I was a teenager and we visited some extended family out of state. I had several cousins who were young boys. These boys couldn't get enough of me; they were always wrestling me, sitting in my lap, holding my hand, even the ones as old as 12. Why? Young boys and girls are naturally attracted to others of the same gender. This is an important stage! They need to be affirmed in their gender identity. My cousins were craving my attention, affection and acceptance because they saw in me what they wanted to be: a big strong guy.

"It's absolutely vital for young boys and girls to receive verbal and physical affirmation and affection from their same-sex mentors. Ideally, by adolescence a boy will have bonded with his father and peers. If this need is not met for a child, it will not go away as he grows but will continue into adolescence. Rather than becoming curious about girls, he will continue to desire male companionship as he becomes sexually mature. Something you will hear almost universally from those who identify as gay is, "I knew I was different since I was little." This is often perceived by the person as proof that they were "born gay." But they weren't aware of their supposed homosexuality as a child; they were feeling the void left by their unmet need to connect with others of their gender.

Very often, a person struggling with same-sex attraction has experienced hurt or rejection instead of acceptance by others of their gender, or simply never made a connection. They might not recall any overt trauma in their childhood (molestation, abuse, abandonment), but the very loss of that connection with their same-gender parent and peers is, in itself, traumatic.

Some strugglers will remember making a conscious choice at some point to reject their gender. They don't decide, "I'm going to be gay" but something more like, "I'm never going to be like dad (or mom)," or, "Pretty girls aren't safe. I don't ever want to be one." This is very common for women struggling with lesbianism. Often they see their mother as weak or endangered (especially if mom is verbally/physically abused). They think it's dangerous to be a woman and embrace those traditional roles, and they promise themselves never to make the same mistake.[4]

I think this brings perspective on the cause of the gay lifestyle. All that I would add is that the devil and his helpers are putting thoughts in people's minds while all of these other factors are working. I'll explain this truth shortly. Further, there are hundreds of thousands of men and women who have embraced the homosexual lifestyle only to abandon it[5] and are happily living as heterosexuals and not struggling at all with the temptation to go back into it.

Another study in 2001 by Dr. Robert L. Spitzer, a Columbia University psychiatry professor, concludes that some gay people can turn straight if they really want to. "Contrary to conventional wisdom, some highly motivated individuals, using a variety of change efforts, can make substantial change in multiple indicators of sexual orientation, and achieve good heterosexual functioning."

> Highly motivated individuals, using a variety of change efforts, can make substantial change in multiple indicators of sexual orientation.

Before the study, Spitzer was a skeptic. He said, "Like most psychiatrists, I thought that homosexual behavior couldn't be resisted, that sexual orientation could not be changed. I now believe that's untrue—some people can and do change."[6]

I really respect the fact that this man was able to stand up and say that he had started his study thinking one way but soon discovered evidence to the contrary. After conducting phone interviews with 200 'ex-gays,' (143 males, 57 females, average age 43), Dr. Spitzer indicated that 66 percent of the men and 44 percent of women had arrived at what he called "good heterosexual functioning." This term was defined as "being in a sustained, loving, heterosexual relationship for the past year and deriving emotional satisfaction from it."

They're saying that seven of ten individuals experience fulfillment and joy in a heterosexual relationship and have satisfying heterosexual relations at least once monthly and never or rarely think of somebody of the same sex during heterosexual sex. In addition 89 percent of the men and 95 percent of the women said they were bothered only slightly or not at all by unwanted homosexual feelings.[7] Only 11 percent of the men and 37 percent of the women reported a complete absence of homosexual indicators including same sex attractions.

This secular study provides concrete evidence that these are folks who were not coming out of the homosexual lifestyle because of Christianity, but because they made a conscious decision to get out of it. And the majority of them reported that psychologists had helped them walk through some of the mental problems and struggles they had dealt with, but were convinced that they are free of it. Now let's look at the spiritual side of the issue.

Paul talks about the devil's kingdom in the New Testament.

> For our struggle *is not against flesh and blood*, **but against the rulers,** *against the authorities, against the powers of this dark world and against the spiritual forces of evil in the heavenly realms.*
> —Ephesians 6:12 (emphasis mine)

In other words, the devil's culture is set up like a hierarchy with Satan as the leader, and under him are secondary helper leaders—various fallen angels—that report to him. Then there are other demons under the secondary leaders, and so on. These levels of leadership have been assigned to every one of us, just as we all received a guardian angel when we were born who has been watching over us since birth. Guardian angels are something to be excited about, not some spying demon! Don't worry, they can't hurt you, but they will try to deceive you by trying to inject false thoughts into your mind!

But since you were born, the devil has assigned what's called a *familiar spirit* or two to you. And they go back and report to their leader who reports to the devil, and they strategize to figure out how they can trip up human beings and cause them to fall into sin. As you study the Bible, you learn they really do have the ability to inject ungodly thoughts into our minds. Here are some examples:

> *The tempter came to him and said, "If you are the Son of God, tell these stones to become bread."*
>
> —Matthew 4:3

Jesus had been led by the Spirit into the desert to be tempted by the devil. He had been fasting for forty days and forty nights. He was hungry. The devil tried to get Jesus to do things that were wrong by injecting thoughts into his mind. Whether or not he appeared to Jesus doesn't matter. The fact that he tempted him by injecting thoughts is what matters. He's trying to do that to all of us today.

Another illustration of the devil's ability to inject thoughts, tempting us to do wrong, can be found in the apostle Paul's writings to the Thessalonians. He wrote to teach them more about Christianity and how to live in order to please God.

> *For this reason, when I could stand it no longer, I sent to find out about your faith. I was afraid that in some way **the tempter might have tempted you and our efforts might have been useless.***
> —1 Thessalonians 3:5 (emphasis mine)

The devil is causing people to believe things that aren't true.

He was concerned about Christians being tempted by demonic forces in the form of thoughts being put in the mind and how they might give in to their sin nature and walk away from Christianity. The devil is doing these things and causing people to believe things that aren't true.

For though we walk in the flesh, we do not war according to the flesh. For the weapons of our warfare are not carnal but mighty in God for pulling down strongholds, <u>casting down arguments and every high thing that exalts itself against the knowledge of God,</u> **bringing every thought into captivity to the obedience of Christ,** *and being ready to punish all disobedience when your obedience is fulfilled.*

—2 Corinthians 10:3-6 NKJV

(emphasis mine)

A Christian won't even recognize an evil thought if they don't know what God's opinion is. They think it's just them. So many homosexuals think they were born that way when in fact, those thoughts have been placed in their minds to work together with negative experiences from the time they were young, and the tempter has tried to get them to fall in that area. Why does the tempter tempt some with homosexual "sex" thoughts and others with heterosexual "sex" thoughts? Maybe we all have propensities toward certain sins and that is the one he hits us with, or maybe our environment sets us up to be tempted in that particular area. Some have a propensity toward substance abuse, so he tempts them in that area. No matter what the reason, it's important to be aware of the source!

Let's look at an environment scenario at this time. I'm going to use young boys as an example, but it could very easily happen in a similar way to a young girl. Some young boys today display effeminate characteristics in their actions. And oftentimes they are made fun of. Some boys are just not interested in sports. They don't want to participate in everything the majority of boys do. Maybe they enjoy some of the things that girls like to do. Perhaps their voice is a couple of octaves higher. These little boys are going into kindergarten, first and second grade, and from the time they walk out of their house, are rejected and made to feel as though they are objects of ridicule. It's painful—it hurts.

Kids are innocent, yes, and they make fun of anything and anyone that's different. They can actually be extremely cruel. So these little boys are singled out at school as targets for bullies. At the same time, little demons are sitting up on their shoulders—the familiar spirits we mentioned—and they're saying, "You are different. You were born that way. You are gay." The demons work hard to convince them of the lie. The devil does it to everyone in one area or another. He tries to get us to believe and do things that, in God's opinion, we shouldn't believe or do.

If you have a child who displays same-sex tendencies, I encourage you to make them feel secure in your love and to let them know it's okay to be different than the majority. Go overboard; work double time, affirming them for who they are. I can assure you the devil is working double time to do the opposite! I like to think of myself as a pretty macho guy, but there are certain things I don't do that a lot of other men like. I don't like fishing. It bores me. I don't like to hunt. You'll never catch me hunting; I don't like it. You know what I like to do? I like to walk around malls and drink "designer" coffee. I like shopping for my wife's clothes. I actually enjoy it. But I'm not gay, I'm Joe! Who are you? Be you without apologizing for it!

We are all guilty of categorizing people, and it's not a good thing to do. We can't put people in a box. God creates all of us differently, and for those little boys and girls who are different, who are we to say that they aren't called to be the next Steven Spielberg or Beethoven? When it comes to boys, they are typically super creative people, and just because they don't fit in with the majority of the population doesn't mean they aren't valuable to the community of humankind. God gave them such strong giftings. When we make fun of them or speak negatively about them, we reinforce the devil's lies that attempt to convince them that their lifestyle choices are by God's design.

We all like and enjoy different things. But it is God who made us, and each of us is uniquely qualified with God-given abilities to do things that others can't do. I want you to know and understand that you are special.

Satan is at work everywhere in the world with everyone in the world. It amazes me that unsaved

> Satan is at work everywhere in the world with everyone in the world.

people are able to walk out of the gay lifestyle by sheer force of their own will. I'm sure that some of them continually resist certain feelings and deal with thoughts because they don't realize the thoughts aren't their own. They don't know the thoughts are not coming from them. They aren't aware of the little demons that were assigned to them from birth.

Earlier in this chapter, I referred to Exodus Global Alliance, a ministry that equips Christians to uphold the biblical view of sexuality. I read their news press release dated April 12, 2005 that says:

> Orlando residents will see two new billboard signs today that feature pictures of former homosexuals who challenge the permanence of homosexuality and offer a message of hope and change. Exodus International [now known as Exodus Global Alliance], the largest network of former homosexuals in the world, sponsored the billboard ads hoping to counter mainstream media messages and offer the

public an … alternative message about homosexuality.

The ads question the immutability of homosexuality and feature seven former homosexuals in the background artwork. [One of the billboards says,] "We questioned homosexuality. Truth brought freedom."

[The other says,] "Rethink homosexuality."

The billboards have already generated local controversy. Originally slated to appear above a local gay resort, the ads were in the process of being put up when the owner protested the content and threatened bodily harm to the crew contracted to post the signs. The ads have since been moved to an alternate site.

Alan Chambers, a former homosexual featured on the billboard and [the current] president of Exodus International responded, "While it is disturbing to see the inconsistency in the gay community's call for tolerance and diversity, our message does not change. Our existence offers hope to others who feel trapped by homosexuality and gives the public a reason to question what they see and hear about this issue every day in the media.

"There are hundreds of thousands of individuals like myself who experienced emptiness and isolation in homosexuality and through Jesus Christ, we found the strength to leave it," said Chambers. "Popular culture says we don't exist, but we do and we want others to hear our stories and consider a side to this issue that they may have never heard before."

Exodus International is a resource and referral organization with over 125 member chapters across North America that offer help to over 400,000 people who contact the ministry each year.

The front and back billboards were up for a year on the east side of US 441, just north of state route 408. The ad was also posted at www.exodusglobalalliance.org.[8]

Why did I read this? Here's a Christian group that's helping people out of that lifestyle, reeducating them and assuring them that they weren't born this way. This is something that they just fell into the same way people fall into a variety of other sins. The message is that you can change the way you live and come out of this. Jesus

Christ can set you free in any area of your life, just as He set me free in other areas.

Highly successful American author and motivational speaker Zig Ziglar tells of a time after he gave a speech. A man came up to him and told him the following, "When I was 10 or 11 years old I told my parents I had homosexual feelings toward other boys. My parents said that they would support me in whatever I chose in life. I entered the homosexual lifestyle until age 60 when I received Jesus Christ as my Savior and Lord. I'm 65 years old now, and the last five years have been the best years of my life. But I can't help thinking about the wife I could have married and the children and grand-children I could have had." Ziglar said that man walked away very, very sad.

Please listen to my heart in this chapter. It is certainly not to condemn anybody. If you have feelings, thoughts, or you've fallen into the homosexual lifestyle, there's good news. God didn't make you or anyone this way. And God can set you free if you want to walk out of the lifestyle.

If you've never accepted Jesus Christ as your Savior—whether or not you're living in the homosexual lifestyle—the Bible says when you accept Christ and place your trust in Him for eternal life, He makes you a new creation, and the old passes away and everything becomes new (see 2 Corinthians 5:17).

You can accept Jesus Christ as your Savior today, and Jesus will literally change you from the inside out. Then as you grow in church and begin to study and learn about God, He will begin to renew your mind, and all those lies that you've been made to believe are going to fall aside. You're going to understand and realize who you are.

If you are a Christian who has fallen into the homo-sexual lifestyle or maybe never walked away from it, I hope that I've helped you understand that you were not born this way. You are not doomed to be this way for the rest of your life. There's a lot of sin out there. And you have to put things in the category that God puts them in. It's wrong for a man to lust after a woman— that's called a sin too. And when a man does it, he has to repent.

The Bible declares that when we repent and tell the Lord we're sorry, He'll wash our sins away. He'll cleanse our souls and begin to minister freedom to every part of our being. And in the darkest, blackest moment, when you think there's no way out, God is holding out His hand, eager to set you free and deliver you forever. I trust that this chapter has been helpful. I trust that it has given you a new perspective and that from this day forward, you

> In the darkest, blackest moment, when you think there's no way out, God is holding out His hand.

will think about this issue in a different way, love those who struggle with it, and let them know that in God there's always deliverance and freedom. The principles we look at in the latter part of this book will help you be free of sin in any area of your life!

God's Opinion in Review
Chapter 7

■ A conclusive medical study conducted by a secular physician at a secular university clearly states the impossibility of determining genetically whether an individual is born a homosexual, because the scientific ability to make that determination doesn't exist.

■ Dr. Joseph Nicolosi's landmark articles for Exodus International, now known as Exodus Global Alliance, focuses light on the subject of what really causes homosexuality, citing seven key factors present in the majority of those who struggle with homosexuality: (1) Absent/distant same-sex parent; (2) Sexual abuse; (3) Bad experience with gender specific activities; (4) Name-calling; (5) Over-involvement with opposite-sex parent; (6) Early exposure to pornography or sexual language; (7) Isolation from same-sex peers.

■ Very often, a person struggling with same-sex attraction has experienced hurt or rejection instead of acceptance by others of their gender, or simply never made a connection. These conditions are a perfect setup for Satan to initiate the process of deceiving the person into believing they're different—probably gay.

∎ Hundreds of thousands of men and women who have embraced the homosexual lifestyle only to abandon it are happily living as heterosexuals and not struggling at all with the temptation to go back into it.

∎ Ephesians 6:12 tells us that our struggles with sin and other issues are not against flesh and blood, but against the powers of evil. The devil plays an enormous role in convincing people that they are gay, that there is no way out of the lifestyle, and that their only shot at happiness is to engage in homosexual relationships because they were born that way.

∎ Jesus was tempted by Satan as we are, yet He did not succumb to the enemy's taunts and lies. The devil can cause people to believe things that are not true, but God, through the power of His Holy Spirit, can reverse all of the devil's lies and set anyone free.

∎ We must not categorize people. God created all of us differently. Just because certain people don't seem to fit in with the majority of the population doesn't mean they aren't valuable to the community of mankind. God made each of us uniquely qualified with God-given abilities to do things that others cannot do. You are special! God himself thinks so!

■ If you have never accepted Christ as your Savior—whether or not you're living in a homosexual lifestyle—the Bible says when you accept Christ and place your trust in Him for eternal life, He makes you a new creation, the old passes away and everything becomes new. You can accept Him today, and Jesus will literally change you from the inside out. As you grow and study and learn about the things of God, He will renew your mind. You will begin to understand who you are. In God there is always deliverance and freedom.

■ Even in the darkest, blackest moment, when you think there is no way out, God is holding out His hand, eager to set you free and deliver you forever.

CHAPTER 8

Abortion,
Pro-Life/
Pro-Choice?

WITHOUT A DOUBT, ABORTION is a very hot topic in this country today—especially during political election seasons. You probably already know this, but on January 22, 1973, the Supreme Court of the United States of America, through a case called Roe v. Wade, legalized abortion in the United States. And since 1973, abortion has been taking place legally in this country of ours. There are two sides to the abortion issue. One is called pro-life, and this faction believes that what a woman is carrying in her womb is an actual child—a life. They believe that this life has rights and should have a voice as to whether or not he or she will live or die. This tiny, little life can't speak for him- or herself, but pro-lifers believe it's a life.

On the other side is what is called pro-choice. This group believes that a woman should have a choice with regard to what she does and does not do upon learning that she is pregnant. Now, I agree that women should have choices. I don't disagree with that at all. But the pro-choice group believes that what's inside a woman's womb is not a life, and since it's not a life, it's fine to go ahead and have an abortion. It is their position that abortion is not really committing murder because the life inside the womb is not a person until the child takes its first breath.

Those are the two sides. And I'll be very honest with you. I think there are really good people on the pro-choice side. I just simply feel that they're misinformed people. And the last thing I want to do is to condemn anybody. I realize that there are many women who are reading this book who have had an abortion. And I want you to understand that the heart of God is not to condemn you. The heart of God is to first help you recognize His part and His will. And when we fail, the heart of God is always for us to repent so He can forgive us, show us His mercy, and bring us closer to Him. So with regard to this subject, I want to make sure that the heart and the mercy of God come through. Near the end of this chapter, I will share some things that I believe will help any woman who has ever had an abortion.

Let's look at some statistics. These statistics are absolutely mind blowing. They are world-wide statistics, not just from the United States of America. The Alan Guttmacher Institute reports

> 46 million abortions are performed legally and illegally worldwide each year.

that approximately 46 million abortions are performed legally and illegally worldwide each year.[1] That is a stunning fact—46 million infants have died. These numbers represent lives—human beings—oh what a lot of lives have been lost!

Here are some other statistics. Some of these surprise me, and you don't hear them in the mainstream media. For instance, abortion is the most frequently performed surgical procedure in the United States of America.[2] This is shocking to me! And The American Medical Association *supports* legislation banning partial birth abortions unless the life of the mother is in danger.[3] I didn't know that. The mainstream media may not publicize this, but the American Medical Association *supports* a ban on partial birth abortions.

The Angus Reid Global Monitor reports that according to a poll conducted by the *New York Times* & *CBS News*, "adults in the United States are split over their country's pregnancy termination guidelines. Thirty-nine percent of those who responded believe abortion should be available to those who want it. [But on the other hand,] 37 percent believe abortion should be available but under stricter limits than it is now, while 21 percent think the procedure should not be permitted."[4]

"A similar poll in January 2006 surveyed people in the United States about U.S. opinion on abortion; 33 percent said that abortion should be 'permitted only in cases such as rape, incest or to save the woman's life,' 27 percent said that abortion should be 'permitted in all cases,' 15 percent that it should be 'permitted, but subject to greater restrictions than it is now,' 17 percent said that it should 'only be permitted to save the woman's life,' and 5 percent said that it should 'never' be permitted."[5]

Currently abortion is legal for any reason in every state of our union. Here's something for the young people. If you haven't already, you should check out the terrific Web site for young people, www.battlecry.com. They report that about a third (34 percent) of young women become pregnant at least once before they reach the age of 20—about 820,000 a year. (Kaiser Family Foundation, January 2005).[6] And that's not a surprise when you consider the message that our teens are taking away from today's media—movies, television sitcoms and dramas, and whatever else. The media is doing nothing less than condoning sex outside of marriage. When you paint that picture for them, show people doing it on television, on the Internet, in the movie theatres, and even on cell phones insinuating that it's being done all the time, what can you expect?

Teen hormones are raging, and the message they receive encourages them to follow suit. I hope this chapter can help teens overcome that. The CDC in reporting trends of teenage pregnancy in the U.S. from 1990-2002 says, "In 2002 an estimated 757,000 pregnancies among teenagers 15-19 years resulted in 425,000 live births, 215,000 induced abortions, and 117,000 fetal losses."[7] And I would venture to say that they have not thought it through and don't understand what they're doing.

The number-one reason for abortions in the United States, according to the Surgeon General from 1982 to 1989, Dr. C. Everett Koop, is convenience. "Abortions in the United States for rape, incest, to protect the life of the mother, or to void a defective fetus comprise less than five percent of all abortions. The rest are performed just for convenience. And we're talking about one million abortions a year."[8]

A 1998 study conducted in twenty-seven countries sought to determine the reasons women seek to end their pregnancies. They concluded that these common factors influenced women to have an abortion:

> Desire to delay or end childbearing
> Concern over interruption of work or education
> Issues of financial or relationship stability
> Perceived immaturity

Concern for health risks posed by pregnancy in individual cases was not a factor commonly given in the United States.

A 2004 study of women who answered questionnaires at clinics in America yielded similar results. One percent of women in this study became pregnant as a result of rape and 0.5 percent as a result of incest.[9]

The Bible teaches that life begins at conception and what's inside of a woman is not just a fetus, but a baby.

To me, if it's such a small percentage that become pregnant from rape and incest, convenience is not a good enough reason for exterminating unborn babies from this planet.

I'm going to do my best to show you that the Bible teaches that life begins at conception and what's inside of a woman is not just a fetus, but a baby. And I want you to pay close attention to these absolutely exceptional scriptures that I will share here. These important scriptures will also confirm to you that you are valuable. This world tries to tell us that we have no value—that if we weren't born into a certain home or family, God has no use for us. It simply is not true.

> **"Before** _I formed you in the womb_ **I knew you, before** _you were born_ **I set you apart;** _I appointed you as a prophet to the nations."_
>
> —Jeremiah 1:5 (emphasis mine)

Wow! God says that He formed us in the womb! He says that he knew us before He formed us in the womb! This truth is true for everyone! We'll talk more about this in a moment. I also like the part of this verse that says, "before you were born, I set you apart." This was God speaking to Jeremiah, a young man called to warn Judah about its sinful lifestyle. In these verses God was giving him the confidence that he would need to respond to the call on his life. In telling Jeremiah that God _knew_ him, He was saying, "I recognize you. My plan for your life was developed before your very life developed in your mother's womb."

Webster defines the word _know_ as "To perceive directly with the senses or mind; to believe to be true with absolute certainty; to have a practical understanding or thorough experience with; to be familiar with; to be cognizant or aware; having knowledge of restricted or secret data."[10] Before you were born (before you took your first breath, God says) I set you apart. I appointed you as a prophet to the nations." Get this. This is not just true for Jeremiah. Isaiah said the same thing. Paul said the same thing of every one of us.

The Bible talks about our calling, and just as God said before Jeremiah was ever born that He had already set him apart, God has set every single one of us apart. We're going to find out in our next scripture that before you took your first breath, God wrote down in a book all the special things He wants you to do on this planet. And He has special assignments for each and every one of us.

It doesn't matter what your natural background is. What matters is what God wrote in His book. We can pray and ask God to reveal to us our purpose for being on this planet. Psalm 139 is one of the best I've ever seen to substantiate God's opinion on when life begins. Let's look at it:

For you [God] ***created my inmost being;***
*   you **knit me together in my mother's womb**.*
I praise you because I am fearfully and wonder-
fully made;
*   your works are wonderful,*
*   I know that full well.*
My frame was not hidden from you
*   when I was made in the secret place.*

When I was woven together in the depths of the earth,

your eyes saw my unformed body.
All the days ordained for me
were written in your book,
before one of them came to be.
—Psalm 139:13-16 (emphasis mine)

Our inmost being is referring to our spirit and soul. We are three-part beings. We are a spirit, we possess a soul, and that spirit and soul live inside our body (see 1 Thessalonians 5:23). We're familiar with our body, of course, but the real us is on the inside. And God said He created the real you and me—our spirit and our soul. So when our parents had relations, do you know what that did? That simply created our body, but God made our spirit. And God does not make anything for naught! The Bible says, "For you created my inmost being. You knit me together in my mother's womb."

I want this to get down deep on the inside of you: God created your spirit and your soul outside of the womb. And when mom and dad conceived, God immediately put your spirit and soul into your body. That's what this section of scripture is saying. The psalmist continues, "I praise you because I am fearfully and wonderfully made; your works are wonderful, I know that full well. My frame was not hidden from you when I was made in the secret place. When I was woven together in the depths of the earth" (vv. 14-15).

Where are the secret place and the depths of the earth? They are not inside momma. From what I can see, God makes our spirit and soul, and He writes in a book what He's called us to do—that's the real us. He decides what body He's going to put it into and at conception, He knits it all together. Now, I don't know about you, but that makes me feel much more valuable. I'm not just Joe who was born to Mr. and Mrs. Cameneti. But I'm also Joe, the one God created and wrote about in a book that records what He wanted me to do on this earth.

God gave all of us something significant and important to do. He said, "All the days ordained for me were written in your book before one of them came to be" (vs. 16). Before we took our first breath, God wrote in the book everything He wanted us to do. God says He created you and formed you in the womb.

How many babies have been aborted whose assignment was to cure the common cold or cancer?

Because of these scriptures, I believe without any doubt that life begins at conception. Before a baby takes his first breath, God already has his life planned out for him. Well, if God has his (or her) life planned out, and He takes a spirit and soul that He created and places it inside the body that came from mom and dad, this has to be a person inside the womb. This got me started to thinking about all of this, and I began to wonder how many babies have been aborted whose assignment was to cure the common cold or cancer? Perhaps their assignment was to solve the hunger problem on this planet... or to be the next Billy Graham or apostle Paul... or the next Ruth Graham or Mother Teresa.

How many of these kids missed the opportunity to fulfill their assignments—their chance to do the extraordinary and excellent things that God created them to do—because they weren't allowed to be born? Maybe the person whom God had designed to discover the cure for AIDS was aborted. How many incredible things could we have been enjoying had these people been given the opportunity to live? I believe this shows us that we're alive when we're inside momma, and we are as much a child there as when we are welcomed to planet earth.

This is a fascinating medical fact: "At conception the embryo is genetically distinct from the mother. To say that the developing baby is no different from the mother's appendix is scientifically inaccurate. A developing embryo is also genetically different from the sperm and egg that created it. A human being has 46 chromosomes. Sperm and egg each have 23 chromosomes. A trained geneticist can now distinguish between the

DNA of an embryo and that of a sperm and an egg. But that same geneticist cannot distinguish between the DNA of a developing embryo and the DNA of a full-grown human being."[11] "From a medical point of view, in the words of a physician, 'The ultimate scientific fact that all [of us] must face and deal with is that nothing, no bits and pieces, will be added to this living human [he's referring to a baby in the womb] from the time of fertilization until the old man dies—nothing except nutrition. Each of us existed in totality at that moment. All that we have done since then is to mature.'"[12]

Again, please realize that my purpose here is not to condemn anybody, but to say that I believe the Bible establishes that life begins at conception and God planned that life out before he or she took a breath. If God did that, then it is a life—something for which you and I should be grateful and about which we must see as precious and valuable. Some things that are going on in this world really clarify where our priorities seem to lie as a nation and contradict God's purpose and plan for the earth, in my estimation.

For example, in the United States, you can be fined $5,000 and imprisoned for up to a year for breaking an eagle's egg.[13] And you can be imprisoned and fined for stealing a sea turtle egg.[14] And yet abortion is legal. Wouldn't an unborn eagle not be an eagle if you used the same rules we're using for what we call a human fetus? Think about it. But scientists say, and this nation concurs, that the eagle in the egg will, in fact, be an eagle at birth, and if the egg is destroyed, an eagle has been destroyed, and that is against the law. The American bald eagle is America's national symbol and is protected by law at the time of this writing. You destroy that egg and you've destroyed an eagle. You're going to pay for that with $5,000 (minimum) from your personal bank account.

Living on the inside of an expectant mother is a human being created in the image of the Creator of the universe. This human being is going to turn into someone not unsimilar to you and me, and God almighty has great plans and desires for this individual.

The Eliot Institute for Social Sciences Research in Springfield, Illinois, was founded in 1988 to perform original research and education on the impact of abortion on women, men, siblings, and society. This group publishes research and educational materials and works as an advocate for women and men seeking post-abortion healing.

One reputable Eliot Institute study, "Psychological Reactions Reported After Abortions," was directed by David C. Reardon, PhD. He asked post-abortion women a variety of questions in a survey-type format with a multiple-choice listing of five response options to the questions. The first choice was (a) Strongly disagree and the last choice was (b) Strongly agree. There were three in between. So I combined the responses from the "Strongly agree" column with the "Agree" column to arrive at the incredible percentages of the responses. You will notice that these poor ladies are hurting and need healing. I believe God can bring healing to them. The statement:

After my abortion I experienced feelings of:

Guilt—92%

Depression—88%

Anger—81%

Sorrow—91%

Bitterness—74%

Regret—85%

Despair—73%

Shame—91%

Hopelessness—73%

Confusion—81%

A general sense of emptiness—83%

Then the women were asked positive questions:

Happiness—8%

Power—6%

Liberation—13%

Sexual freedom—15%

Inner peace—5%

More in control of my life—7%[15]

But the picture that's painted for you and me in the media is that because they have a choice, there's great liberation. These statistics refute that claim. Wouldn't you think, as I do, that "great liberation" should produce happiness, power, sexual freedom, and inner peace? If these statistics are correct, it seems that this "great liberation" brings only sadness, regret, and shame.

> A life was killed through the abortion, and that is a heavy burden to try and work through.

Seventy-one percent said their memory of the abortion remains vividly clear. When asked if they had ever regretted having an abortion, 94 percent said yes.[16] I think these statistics confirm the reason the women come away from this experience with feelings of guilt and sadness. I believe they realize that a life was killed through the abortion, and that is a heavy burden to try and work through. And let me go on to say that I think we have to understand the standard of God. I believe that God is saying there is life in the womb. And even those who don't believe it's a living person need to examine the results of this study and understand what these precious women feel. There's a reason for it.

The good news is that there is a God in heaven who can restore and forgive those who have suffered through the decision to have an abortion and then gone through with it. If this is you (your daughter, your niece, your granddaughter, your neighbor's teenage daughter, or your daughter's college roommate), and you're not a Christian (and you know they are not), I encourage you to give your heart to Jesus. Let Jesus take your soul, wash it, and cleanse it. He will wash away all those feelings, and the Bible says when we give our life to Christ that He forgives us of all our sins.

If you are a Christian who has had an abortion and now experience feelings of guilt, shame, and regret—if you're one of the 94 percent who say they wish they had never done it—the Bible says if we confess our sins, God is faithful and just to forgive us. He's faithful and just to cleanse us, and I like this part, He cleanses us from *all* unrighteousness.

Do you know what that means? He cleans up our soul and restores to us His peace and joy. We're no longer empty and full of shame. I hope that you hear my heart, and I hope that through my heart you're feeling the heart of God. Understanding the heart of God is real simple. All of us have sinned, all of us have fallen short of His glory, but in Christ Jesus, there's forgiveness. As we admit we sinned and made a mistake, God promises to forgive us and wipe our soul clean. I—along with a multitude of Christians—will pray for your restoration!

From this day forward, I urge you to join me in praying for the current unborn children and for the women who have to make a decision to abort them.

Pray that this nation will change its stance on abortion. And pray that these children will live, because I believe we're losing some of our greatest leaders and most important people. They aren't given the chance to take their first breath, and God designed big plans for them.

God's Opinion in Review
Chapter Eight

▌ The two sides to the abortion issue in the U.S. are known as "Pro-Life" and "Pro-Choice." The pro-lifers believe that an expectant mother is carrying an actual infant child in her womb—a life; a little person—who has rights and should have a voice as to whether or not he or she will live or die. The pro-choice group believes that a woman should have a choice with regard to what she does and does not do upon learning that she is pregnant. (This includes a choice of abortion.)

▌ The heart of God is not to condemn anyone who has had an abortion, but God's heart is to help women recognize His part and His will. The mercy of God is there for anyone who repents of their sin.

▌ Statistics show that approximately 46 million abortions are performed legally and illegally each year worldwide. Forty-six million infants have died as a result of abortion!

▌ Americans are split over their country's pregnancy termination guidelines. Thirty-nine percent of those who responded to a survey believe abortion should be available to those who want it. On the other hand, 37 percent believe abortion should be available but under stricter limits than it is now, while 21 percent think the procedure should not be permitted.

▮ Abortion is currently legal for any reason in every state of the 50 United States of America. There is a very helpful Web site for young people, **www. battlecry.com**, which reports that 34 percent of young women become pregnant at least once before the age of 20—about 820,000 a year!

▮ The number-one reason for abortions in America, according to a former U.S. Surgeon General, is convenience. Studies show that a very small number of women have an abortion as a result of rape or incest.

▮ The Old Testament book of Jeremiah confirms in chapter one that God actually said He formed us in the womb, that He knew us before we were even born, and set us apart for himself.

▮ Psalm 139 is one of the best verses in the Bible with regard to substantiating God's opinion on when life begins. And 1 Thessalonians 5:23 unequivocally states that we are a spirit, we possess a soul, and that spirit and soul live in our body. Our parents' union created our physical body, but God made our spirit outside of the womb. When mom and dad conceived, God immediately put your spirit and soul into your body.

■ Before a baby takes his first breath, God already has his life planned out for him. How many babies have been aborted whose assignment was to cure the common cold or cancer, heart disease or diabetes?

■ It is clear, from the Word of God, that life begins at conception, and God had specific plans for that life before he or she took a breath. If God did that, then it is a life for which you and I should be grateful and about which we must see as precious and valuable.

■ Statistics reveal that great numbers of women who have had abortions experienced enormous guilt, depression, anger, sorrow, bitterness, regret, despair, shame, hopelessness, confusion, and a general sense of emptiness. Very few of those polled experienced happiness, power, liberation, sexual freedom, inner peace, or a sense that they were more in control of their lives.

■ More than 70 percent of the survey respondents said their memory of the abortion remains vividly clear, even years later. The sadness, in other words, doesn't just go away for most women.

▌ God can clean up our soul and restore us to a place of peace and joy. When we give our life to Christ, He forgives all of our sins, including abortion. He is faithful and just to forgive us and cleanse us of all unrighteousness.

Sin Stained?

I WANT TO DEDICATE THE REMAINDER of this book to two things: Understanding what we, as Christians, must do to conquer sin, and how we should treat those who aren't Christians who live in and practice sin. I think the best place to start is for us to realize how we're born into this earth and why we can't go to heaven unless we accept Jesus. Clearly understanding this truth will prepare us to conquer sin and treat sinners correctly! I've spoken with many people over the years who, like me, came to Christ after living sinful lives as non-Christians. At that time we were blind to what we were doing and, in most cases, didn't even feel guilt. We didn't realize that what we were doing was not pleasing to God. Many people in the world live, play, and enjoy their lives without having even the slightest clue that they're living in bondage to sin. The hot sexual topics of the day that we have discussed in this book—from sexual fantasizing, viewing Internet pornography, and unfaithfulness to homosexuality and abortion—mean nothing to them, as wrong as it is to those of us who try our best to adhere to traditional Judeo-Christian values and train up our children in the way they should go. The world does not view these topics we have been discussing as sin at all. It's completely normal to the unbeliever. What's the big deal?

It is a big deal to us because we realize that people in our world—even people we know—are trapped in sin. They seem to have no idea as to how far they have strayed from morality, decency, ethics, virtue or integrity. Really, it's because of their nature—who they are on the inside. Only accepting Christ can change that for them.

The apostle Paul shares many important truths in the Bible. He makes it very clear in a letter he wrote to the Roman Christians and another letter he wrote to the Christians in Ephesus that every person born on planet earth is sin stained—that their very nature is a sin nature.

*When Adam sinned, **sin entered the entire human race**. Adam's sin brought*

*death, so death spread to everyone, **for everyone sinned.***
　　　—Romans 5:12 NLT (emphasis mine)

*Once you were dead, doomed forever because of your many sins. **You used to live just like the rest of the world, full of sin**.... All of us used to live that way, following the passions and desires of our evil nature... **We were born with an evil nature**....*
　　　—Ephesians 2:1-3 NLT (emphasis mine)

According to the Bible, God's word to mankind, sin is part of mankind's DNA. We are literally stained with it. We're born that way because of Adam's sin. When he sinned, from that moment on, every time a baby was born they were born sin stained, with what the Bible calls an evil nature. These are, at least at first, good people who don't know the state they're born into. It's kind of like they were born into chapter 15 of a 20-chapter novel, and they don't have a clue of what happened in chapters 1–14. That's where we, the Christians, have to help make people aware and let them know what happened in chapter one when Adam sinned! Understanding this truth also explains why people who don't accept Jesus can't go to heaven. Allow me to begin to explain this awesome truth.

Isaiah provides some insight into the matter:

> *In the year King Uzziah died, I saw the Lord. He was sitting on a lofty throne, and the train of his robe filled the Temple. Hovering around him were mighty seraphim, each with six wings. With two wings they covered their faces, with two they covered their feet, and with the remaining two they flew. In a great chorus they sang,* **"Holy, holy, holy is the LORD Almighty!** *The whole earth is filled with his glory!" The glorious singing shook the Temple to its foundations, and the entire sanctuary was filled with smoke. Then I said, "My destruction is sealed, for* **I am a sinful man and a member of a sinful race.** *Yet I have seen the King, the LORD Almighty!"*
> —Isaiah 6:1-5 NLT (emphasis mine)

If we—in our sinful state—were to see the Lord, we would probably say exactly the same thing: "I'm doomed." We would immediately recognize our sinful state. And that's what happened to Isaiah. When he saw God in all His goodness and glory, and saw the angelic beings singing, "Holy, holy, holy is the Lord Almighty," he immediately realized what was wrong with him. He realized that he was sin stained. That word *holy* is translated the same in both the Old and New Testaments, whether it's from the Hebrew or the Greek. It means, "Number one; to be sacred." God certainly fits that description. There's no doubt about it.

> There is no sin in God—He's 100 percent free from the pollutants of sin.

But the word *holy* also means, "To be free from pollutants." And in context, we could accurately say it this way: "To be free from the pollutants of sin." There is no sin in God—He's 100 percent free from the pollutants of sin. This word can also be translated "clean." So God is number one, sacred, free from the pollutants of sin, and clean. And mankind is sin stained, dirty, and trapped in sin. Allow me to further prove this point.

> *God is light and there is no darkness in him at all.*
>
> —1 John 1:5 NLT

The great scientific minds of our day tell us that darkness is not a substance—it is nothing more than the absence of light. And you can only have darkness if light is not present. The Bible says God is light and no darkness exists in Him—there is just not any darkness in the Lord. I don't know where you are right now, but if you're reading this book, you are probably sitting in a comfortable chair where there is a nice reading light close by. The entire room is not bright with light in my office where I am writing at the moment, but there is a light very near to where I am working. My office is illuminated with a combination of man-made light and some natural light from the windows, but God is perfect light—pure light—and there is not one ounce of darkness in Him. He is holy and wholly free from the pollutants of sin that we discussed in an earlier chapter.

Another description of God can be found in 1 John:

> *But anyone who does not love does not know God—for God is love.*
> —1 John 4:8 NLT

God is love, pure love. You will find no hatred, envy or jealousy in God, because He is 100 percent love. He's pure light, He's holy, and He loves completely. Remember, we're sin stained. Are you beginning to figure out there is a problem? Holy God. Sin-stained man!

Because God is holy and we're sin stained, we can't enter into His presence and live. We can't enjoy God's company and survive His holiness. Here's a scriptural example: Moses got to be really close with God the

Father and they enjoyed an extraordinary relationship, but it could only go so far. Let's look in the book of Exodus:

> Moses said to the LORD, "You have been telling me, 'Take these people up to the Promised Land.' But you haven't told me whom you will send with me. You call me by name and tell me I have found favor with you. Please, if this is really so, show me your intentions so I will understand you more fully and do exactly what you want me to do. Besides, don't forget that this nation is your very own people." And the LORD replied, "I will personally go with you, Moses. I will give you rest—everything will be fine for you." Then Moses said, "If you don't go with us personally, don't let us move a step from this place. If you don't go with us, how will anyone ever know that your people and I have found favor with you? How else will they know we are special and distinct from all other people on the earth?"
>
> And the LORD replied to Moses, "I will indeed do what you have asked, for you have found favor with me, and you are my friend." Then Moses had one more request.

> *"Please let me see your glorious presence,"*
> *he said.* <u>*The* Lord *replied*</u>*, "I will make all*
> *my goodness pass before you, and I will call*
> *out my name, 'the* Lord*,' to you. I will show*
> *kindness to anyone I choose, and I will show*
> *mercy to anyone I choose.* **<u>But you may not</u>**
> **<u>look directly at my face, for no one may see</u>**
> **<u>me and live.</u>** *" The* Lord *continued, "Stand*
> *here on this rock beside me. As my glorious*
> *presence passes by, I will put you in the cleft*
> *of the rock and cover you with my hand*
> *until I have passed.* **Then I will remove my**
> **hand, and you will see me from behind.**
> **But my face will not be seen."**
> —Exodus 33:12-23 NLT (emphasis mine)

If you and I were to see God face-to-face in our sinful state, we would die. And that's what He just said.

> If you and I were to see God face-to-face in our sinful state, we would die.

Sin cannot live in the presence of God, because God is absolute holiness, absolute light, and absolute love. So is God going to forbid us to go to heaven because he doesn't want us to dirty it up?

I have six brothers, so there are seven boys in our family. We had no sisters. When we were young we loved to play tackle football with all of our neighborhood friends, and sometimes we played in the rain and immediately after it had rained. When you play in the mud, you get pretty dirty. When we came home in that condition, our mom would scream out the window, "Boys, don't even come in the house! Get the hose and rinse off." And we rinsed each other off with the hose in the back yard. Then we had to go into the garage, rinse off some more in there, undress to our Skivvies and rinse everything, and then put our clothes into a plastic bag.

Then we went downstairs, threw the clothes into the washer, and jumped into the shower. My mom didn't want any dirt in her house. As a parent, I'm the same way. But God isn't looking at you and me this way. He is not looking down here and saying, "I don't want you to come into heaven because you're going to mess it up with your sin-stained self. You're just going to track up heaven with your messes!" No! God can't allow us into heaven because He is perfect holiness, light, and love and we can't exist in His presence.

I like the way that Paul describes us in the book of Romans.

> For **all have sinned**; <u>**all fall short**</u> of
> God's glorious standard.
> —Romans 3:23 NLT (emphasis mine)

Now, we know we have sinned because we're born with sin. We're sin stained. You may be thinking, *Hey, Pastor Joe, I'm not that bad a person.* I agree. There are many people in the world who, even though they're sin stained, aren't murderers or bank robbers, or porn stars, etc. But, we still have a sin nature and we do sin, whether it's the big ones or the little ones! I think of both of my grandmothers—two of the sweetest people on planet earth. My mom's mom came over to our house every Sunday and brought a gallon of ice cream, hard Italian cookies, and veal cutlets. And every Sunday mom would fry up Grandma's cutlets and put them on the table along with her pasta, meatballs, sausage, Italian green beans, etc., to feed seven hungry boys. I have great memories of my mom's mom.

And we'd go to my dad's mom's house. We called her Nana. She had every type of candy bar ever made, homemade blueberry and apple pies, and food galore. I can't even imagine that my sweet little grandmas ever did anything really all that bad, but they also were sin stained from birth. Even my sweet grandmas fell short of God's glorious standard, and that's why God sent His Son to help us out. That's why Jesus came, because we were doomed. Have you ever thought of it this way? You and I can't go to heaven because we're sin stained.

Think about this. When we die, there are only two places to go. One is heaven, and the other is called hell.

We also call it the lake of fire. God did not create the lake of fire for any human being. It was created for the devil and all the angels that joined in his rebellion against God. It was never intended for one human being to spend one second in hell. Whenever a human being dies without having trusted in Jesus, they're sin stained, and they can't go to heaven. There's only one other place to go, and I can guarantee you from reading the Scriptures, it grieves the heart of God every time one human being has to be sent to the lake of fire.

What God really wants for us—what He created Adam and Eve to do and to be—is to be with Him forever in His presence. But something separates us, and it's the sin stain. That's why Jesus was sent—to take care of this sin stain that was on us. Only He can set us free from our sin stain.

> *My dear children, I am writing this to you so that you will not sin. But if you do sin, there is someone to plead for you before the Father. He is Jesus Christ, the one who pleases God completely. He is the sacrifice for our sins.* ***He takes away not only our sins but the sins of all the world.***
> —1 John 2:1-2 NLT (emphasis mine)

When Jesus was hung on the tree, the Bible declares that God placed the sins of the whole world on him. So every sin—small or big, sexual or non-sexual—was placed on Jesus. He carried the guilt of all of it. I love

Every sin—small or big, sexual or non-sexual—was placed on Jesus.

this! Jesus takes away all the sins. He doesn't just take ours, but those of the whole world. And God is waiting for every person on planet earth to trust in Jesus so they can

become His and He can wipe away their sins. Jesus is in the sin-cleaning business. That's what He does. That's why He came. His sacrifice made us worthy of God, so we would come up to His holy standard.

The New Testament book of Hebrews says it all:

The old system in the Law of Moses was only a shadow of the things to come, not the reality of the good things Christ has done for us. The sacrifices [animal sacrifices in the Old Testament] *under the old system were repeated again and again, year after year, **but they were never able to provide perfect cleansing for those who came to worship**. If they could have provided perfect cleansing, the sacrifices would have stopped, for the worshipers would have been purified* once for all time, and their feelings of guilt would have disappeared.

But just the opposite happened. Those yearly sacrifices reminded them of their sins year after year. For it is not possible for the blood of bulls and goats to take away sins. That is why Christ, when he came into the world, said,

"You did not want animal sacrifices and grain offerings.

But you have given me a body so that I may obey you.

No, you were not pleased with animals burned on the altar

or with other offerings for sin.

Then I said, 'Look, I have come to do your will, O God—

just as it is written about me in the Scriptures.'"

Christ said, "You did not want animal sacrifices or grain offerings or animals burned on the altar or other offerings for sin, nor were you pleased with them" (though they are required by the law of Moses). Then he added, "Look, I have come to do your will." He cancels the first covenant in order to establish the second. **And what God wants**

> *is for us to be made holy by the sacrifice of*
> *the body of Jesus Christ once for all time.*
> —Hebrews 10:1-10 NLT (emphasis mine)

We have been made holy by trusting in Jesus. Look at how Paul says it in Colossians:

> *For God in all his fullness was pleased to live in Christ, and by him God reconciled everything to himself. He made peace with everything in heaven and on earth by means of his blood on the cross. **This includes you who were once so far away from God.** You were his enemies, separated from him by your evil thoughts and actions, yet now he has brought you back as his friends. He has done this through his death on the cross in his own human body. As a result, he has brought you into the very presence of God, **and you are holy and blameless as you stand before him without a single fault.***
> —Colossians 1:19-22 NLT (emphasis mine)

When you and I accepted Christ, He removed the sin stain that we were born into. We're holy! Did you know that once you accept Christ as your Savior that you become as holy as God is? I didn't say we're part of the godhead or that we're little gods! But holy is holy! God, through Jesus, makes you and me holy, just as He is holy! We have to learn to walk in this holiness, but in His sight we are holy and blameless! According to the Bible, those who accept Christ and trust in Him for eternal life have been brought up to the very presence of God, in the spirit realm, of course. We're seated together in heavenly places with Christ Jesus, which enables us to walk free from sin and go to heaven when we die!

When you and I accept Christ on the inside, our spirit man is absolutely 100 percent changed and created in the image and likeness of Jesus.

> *Therefore, if anyone is in Christ* [this happens when we accept Christ], **he is a new creation;** *the old has gone, the new has come! God made him who had no sin to be sin for us, so that in him* **we might become the righteousness of God.**
> —2 Corinthians 5:17, 21 (emphasis mine)

The Bible says we are created in the image and likeness of God almighty. Our spirit man is 100 percent holy but we still have a sin nature in our bodies, and Christians can sin as easily as non-Christians if we don't place certain laws into motion, which we'll discuss shortly. No need to remain sin stained!

God's Opinion in Review
Chapter 9

▌ Clearly understanding the truth that we all must conquer sin in our own lives, that we must not mistreat people who live in and practice sin, and that we won't go to heaven when we die unless we accept Jesus will prepare us to work at overcoming sin and treating sinners correctly.

▌ Multitudes of people are trapped in sin. They have no idea as to how far they have strayed from morality, decency, ethics, virtue, or integrity. Only accepting Christ can change that for them. We are all sin stained—it is part of our DNA.

▌ The Bible says that God is light and in Him there is no darkness at all (1 John 1:5). God is also love, according to 1 John 4:8—anyone who does not love does not know God for God is love. There is no envy or jealousy in God, because he is 100 percent love. He is pure light, holiness, and He loves completely. We have a problem since we are sin stained and God is holy. We cannot enter into His presence and enjoy His company with the stain of sin in our lives. We would actually die if we were to see God face-to-face in our sinful state.

▋ The Good News is that though all have sinned and fallen short of the glory of God, He compensated for that in the death and resurrection of His Son, Jesus Christ, sent to be our Savior and cover our multitude of sins with His precious blood and make us white as snow! Why? Because God really wants us to be forever with Him. He really wants nothing whatsoever to separate us from Him. Jesus took care of this sin stain that was on us and only He can set us free.

▋ Every sin—large or small, sexual or non-sexual—was placed on Jesus. He carried the guilt of it all. He is in the sin-cleaning business. That's why He came. His sacrifice made us worthy of God, so we could come up to His holy standard.

▋ When we accept Christ as Savior, He removes the sin stain that we were born into. We're holy! We have to learn to walk in this holiness, but in the sight of God, we are actually holy and blameless! We are seated together in heavenly places with Christ Jesus—enabled to walk free from sin and go to heaven when we die!

▌ Our spirit man is 100 percent holy, but we still have a sin nature in our body, and Christians can sin as easily as non-Christians if we don't place into motion certain laws that God has set forth in His Word—again, God's opinion.

Conquering Sin!

A 2001 SURVEY PUBLISHED IN *Leadership Journal* states that "37 percent of pastors said pornography was a struggle for them, and 51 percent admitted it was a temptation. 'For 25 years, I would have said that the pro-life issue is the most pressing threat to America morally, but pornography has overtaken it,' said the Rev. Richard Land, a prominent leader in the Southern Baptist Convention, the largest US Protestant denomination. 'More people's lives are being destroyed on a daily basis by addiction to pornography than through abortion.'"[1] Christians struggling with all kinds of sin is a major issue! If pastors, our spiritual leaders—who are trying their best to serve God—are struggling with pornography, then how difficult is it for the average Christian to overcome sin and walk free?

Christians who aren't applying biblical principles to their lives struggle in exactly the same way as non-Christians do.

What happens when Christians know they are doing something wrong, but they continue to struggle with it? We tell the Lord we're sorry, and then we struggle with it some more. What can we do to overcome sin—whether it's sexual or any other type of sin? God has an opinion about this subject, and in this chapter, we're going to find out exactly what He has to say about Christians who struggle with sin.

In all my years of ministry, I've noticed that Christians who aren't applying biblical principles to their lives struggle in exactly the same way as non-Christians do. They are struggling because of what we talked about in our previous chapter. Their sin stain has been removed from their spirit (the real them), but it does still live in their mortal bodies. Our bodies won't be changed until Jesus comes back. When He returns, we'll receive what the Bible calls a glorified body, and it will not have a sin nature. While we're here, as we'll see, we have to supersede that sin nature in our bodies. Because it's there, it can seem as if we have a dual nature, two parts of us fighting for supremacy in our everyday life. Even the apostle Paul had this problem.

> *What I don't understand about myself is* <u>*that I decide one way,*</u> **but then I act another,** *doing things* **I absolutely despise.** *But I need something more! For if I know the law* [what God says is right or wrong] **but still can't keep it,** *and if the power of sin within me keeps sabotaging my best intentions, I obviously need help! I realize that I don't have what it takes. I can will it,* **but I can't do it.** *I decide to do good, but I don't really do it;* <u>*I decide not to do bad,*</u> **but then I do it anyway.** *My decisions, such as they are, don't result in actions. Something has gone wrong deep within me and gets the better of me every time. … The moment I decide to do good,* <u>*sin is there to trip me up.*</u> *I truly* <u>*delight in God's commands,*</u> *but it's pretty obvious that not all of me joins in that delight. Parts of me covertly rebel, and just when I least expect it, they take charge.*
> —Romans 7:15, 17-23 THE MESSAGE
> (emphasis mine)

We all struggle this way, even after we accept Christ, because of our dual nature. I'll share with you how we can overcome this dual nature as we progress, but it is because of our dual nature that many Christians are trapped in sin, just like non-Christians. Because they don't know how to overcome sin, they remain trapped. I'm going to share a story about the life of Samson, the strongest man who ever lived on planet earth. His strength was a result of living a holy, separated life unto God.

Samson's history is detailed in the Old Testament book of Judges 13-16. Even some non-Christians know the story about his long hair being the source of Samson's unmatched strength. In this context, I will present what I call the five levels of sin and demonstrate how Samson, like many of us, can fall into every one of these stages. We can learn much from his very symbolic life that remains relevant even today. Let's look at the five stages of sin:

1. The seduction stage
2. The satisfaction stage
3. The synchronization stage
4. The shamelessness stage
5. The subjugation stage

From birth Samson was known as a Nazirite. An angel of the Lord appeared to his mother and declared, "Indeed now, you are barren and have borne no children, but you shall conceive and bear a son. Now therefore, please be careful not to drink wine or similar drink, and not to eat any unclean thing. For behold, you shall conceive and bear a son. And no razor shall come upon his head, for the child shall be a Nazirite to God from the womb; and he shall begin to deliver Israel out of the hand of the Philistines (Judges 13:3-5 NKJV).

Typically, a Nazirite was a person who took a vow for a month, two months, and sometimes even a year that they were separating themselves unto God—just as you and I are called to be sacred and separated unto God. There were certain rules that the Nazirites had to follow. Breaking these rules was equivalent to us sinning. These were the rules that had to be followed:

1. A Nazirite could not cut his hair. Samson's legendary strength didn't actually come from his hair, but from the Nazirite vow of separation. His hair was symbolic of the vow that he had taken.

2. He could not drink wine or other fermented drinks.

3. He could not eat grapes or anything made from the vine, such as grape juice, vinegar, etc.

4. He could not go near a dead body—human or animal. That was considered symbolic of sin. If a Nazirite came across a dead body, even if he was walking with someone who dropped dead while they were walking along, the Nazirite was required to submit to a cleansing ceremony which included the shaving of his head.

5. He could not eat anything unclean: pork, shellfish, etc.

6. He had to obey the Mosaic Law like everyone else.

The difference with Samson was the length of time he committed to his vow—it was for a lifetime. Otherwise, Samson and others who took the vow were subject to the typical things that were required of any Jew. But then they had some specific things. And we'll talk about that as we progress.

The Bible will serve to introduce us to the seduction stage:

As Samson and his parents were going down to Timnah, a young lion attacked

> *Samson near the vineyards of Timnah. At*
> *that moment the <u>Spirit of the LORD power-*
> *fully took control of him</u>, and* **he ripped the**
> **lion's jaws apart with his bare hands.** *He*
> *did it as easily as if it were a young goat. <u>But*
> *he didn't tell his father or mother about it.</u>*
> —Judges 14:5-6 NLT (emphasis mine)

I think it's interesting that 1 Peter 5:8 in the New Testament tells us that the devil walks around as a roaring lion seeking whom he may devour. I don't think it's by chance that a lion came out to attack Samson instead of a bear or some other animal. God was trying to teach us something with this story. The lion is a type of temptation to sin that we all face. Remember, Samson wasn't allowed to come into contact with a dead animal or human. If he did he would have to shave his head and go through a cleansing process, even if it was the result of an accident. So now he'd killed a lion. It's dead! He should have submitted to the cleansing process and he didn't. He didn't tell his parents because I'm sure Momma would have made him go through the cleansing!

This first incident is the seduction stage. It's the same as you and I being tempted to sin, falling into the temptation, and not repenting of it. The result of this will always open the door for us to go to the next level of sin, the satisfaction stage.

My goal as we go on into this book is to show you how to conquer temptation and sin. Should it ever get the best of you and you fall into sin, you must repent and confess your sin to God! If you don't, you'll enter into stage two, the satisfaction stage of sin.

> *Later, when he returned to Timnah for the wedding, <u>he turned off the path</u> **to look at the carcass of the lion.** And he found that a swarm of bees had made some honey in the carcass. <u>He scooped some of the honey into his hands and ate it along the way.</u> He also gave some to his father and mother, and they ate it. <u>But he didn't tell them</u> he had taken **the honey from the carcass of the lion.***
>
> —Judges 14:8-9 NLT (emphasis mine)

Now Samson was returning to the same sin he didn't repent of the last time! He made a conscious effort to sin. I believe God had placed that bee hive in the carcass of the dead lion to teach us something. Honey is sweet. It tastes good. When we don't repent after being tempted in the seduction stage and follow through with the sin, we're bound to enter stage two where sin becomes fun and enjoyable—not to our spirit, but to the sin nature in our bodies. Sin is now satisfying!

God doesn't want any of us to be in this stage. You can break out of whatever stage you might be hanging out in. And you can go to a level where you're able to conquer sin no matter where you are in your spiritual journey. Unfortunately, there are so many Christians living in this satisfaction stage of sin. Living here for long leads to the next level.

> You can go to a level where you're able to conquer sin no matter where you are in your spiritual journey.

The next level—the synchronization level—is extremely dangerous. Samson has been captured by the Philistines—the enemy from whom God had called him to deliver Israel.

> As Samson arrived at Lehi, the Philistines came shouting in triumph. <u>But the Spirit of the Lord powerfully took control of Samson,</u> and he snapped the ropes on his arms as if they were burnt strands of flax, and they fell from his wrists. Then **he picked up a donkey's jawbone** that was lying on the ground <u>and killed a thousand Philistines with it.</u>
>
> —Judges 15:14-15 NLT (emphasis mine)

Notice this. God is still working with him here, and God will work with us in all three of the early stages of sin, but here's why I call it the synchronization stage. He grabbed the jawbone of a dead donkey—something he was forbidden to touch as a Nazirite. Hello! Samson was now so used to sin that he could practice it and continue to do his ministry! I think it's fascinating that on one hand he had sinned (that's what the dead jawbone represents). And on the other hand, he's fulfilling the call of God on his life to deliver Israel from the Philistines! That's why I call this the synchronization stage. If you play with sin too long, don't repent and learn to conquer it, you'll eventually come to a place where it's synchronized into your life, and you're able to do ministry and sin at the same time. You're able to do ministry and be in the house of God, work for God, and sin at the same time.

And we can become so comfortable with sin that we become hardened in our conscience without even realizing that we have this or that sin in our lives. Samson had the anointing and power of God on him. He could have defeated all one thousand of the Philistines with his bare hands. He did not need the jawbone of a donkey to do it, but he chose to pick up what was sin for him. He became so comfortable with sin, it was easy to do. Are you able to partake of pornography on Saturday night and worship God on Sunday morning, or work in the church on Sunday morning? These things should not be. They're not normal! But the heart of God is for Christians to have no pollutants of sin in their lives—we are to be holy people and walk a holy and awesome life on planet earth. Are you living in this stage? If so, today is the day to make a decision to walk free!

The next stage is a scary one. I call it the shamelessness stage. And in this stage, you begin to sin big time. Let's look at what the Bible says about the shamelessness stage.

> *One day Samson went to the Philistine city of Gaza and spent the night with a prostitute.*
>
> —Judges 16:1 NLT

Isn't that fascinating? Just like that he went out and spent the night with a prostitute. This literally broke the Law of Moses. No one in Israel—no Jew—was allowed to sleep with a prostitute. Notice something here. This sin did not begin with the shamelessness stage. It started way back at the seduction stage when Samson ignored the required cleansing rites after touching the dead animal carcass. Then it went to the satisfaction stage, followed by the synchronization stage. Now, all of a sudden, he committed a major sin.

Sometimes when you commit the big sins, God uncovers it and you're shamed. It ruins your reputation and your ministry (if you're in ministry). Sometimes it seems as though you've gotten away with it, but then you enter into the next stage, and that's the stage where sin literally destroys your life.

> When Christians learn to walk holy and conquer sin, we won't find sin acceptable in ourselves or others.

In the '80s the world witnessed the fall of several well-known television evangelists. Similar incidents have recently happened again. None of those leaders just decided one day to go out and commit these sins. They progressively grew into that place. Their conscience became numb and callused. When temptation came along, they had no trouble falling into it. God doesn't want any of us to be in this stage.

When Christians learn to walk holy and conquer sin, we won't find sin acceptable in ourselves or others. We will come to abhor sin as God abhors sin—not the sinner but the sin. The world we live in won't know what to do with us because we'll look and act so differently as we love sinners and help them to resist sin.

I believe God is calling us to a place where the spirit of Phinehas is in our midst. Phinehas may not be a Bible character that comes to mind instantly even among lifelong Christians. Many unbelievers are somewhat familiar with Moses or Joshua, Peter or Paul, but Phinehas isn't as well known. He was actually a great-nephew of Moses.

Let's get acquainted with Phinehas and compare his morals to those of Israel as recorded in the Old Testament book of Numbers:

> *While the Israelites were camped at Acacia, some of the men **defiled themselves by sleeping with the local Moabite women.** These women invited them to attend sacrifices to their gods, and soon the Israelites were feasting with them and worshiping the gods of Moab. Before long Israel was joining in the worship of Baal of Peor, causing the Lord's anger to blaze against his people. The Lord issued the following command to Moses: "Seize all the ringleaders and execute them before the Lord in broad daylight, so his fierce anger will turn away from the people of Israel." So Moses ordered Israel's judges to execute everyone who had joined in worshiping Baal of Peor.*
>
> *<u>Just then one of the Israelite men brought a Midianite woman into the camp,</u> right before the eyes of Moses and all the people, as they were weeping at the entrance of*

the Tabernacle [meeting house]. **When Phinehas son of Eleazar and grandson of Aaron the priest saw this,** *he jumped up and left the assembly. Then* <u>*he took a spear and rushed after the man into his tent.*</u> **Phinehas thrust the spear all the way through the man's body and into the woman's stomach.** *So the plague against the Israelites was stopped, but not before 24,000 people had died.*

Then the Lord said to Moses, "Phinehas son of Eleazar and grandson of Aaron the priest has turned my anger away from the Israelites by displaying passionate zeal among them on my behalf. So I have stopped destroying all Israel as I had intended to do in my anger.

So tell him that **I am making my special covenant of peace with him.** *In this covenant,* **he and his descendants will be priests for all time, because he was zealous for his God** *and made atonement for the people of Israel."*

—Numbers 25:1-13 NLT (emphasis mine)

Please do not misunderstand me. I do not believe that God wants us to be judgmental, but I really believe God is creating many Phinehases at this distinct time in history—people who have a spirit of holiness on them and believe it is vitally important to live a clean and holy life. Can you see how important Phinehas's stand against blatant sin in the eyes of God was? More than 24,000 died as a result of their sin!

Unfortunately, Samson had no Phinehas to prick his conscience. There was nobody strong enough to rein him in. We find no evidence of anyone who seemed to be willing to step up and point out that he was violating his Nazirite vows to God. So he went through the five stages of sin without anyone attempting to help him stop. He quickly went from the seduction stage to shamelessness, but then he found himself in the subjugation stage, and that's when lives are destroyed. It's the stage of sin where the person is put into bondage, spiritual slavery!

Later Samson fell in love with a woman named Delilah, who lived in the valley of Sorek. It is fascinating to me that the name of Delilah's hometown, Sorek, means "the vines." By Nazirite rules, Samson was to go nowhere near grapes or fruit of the vine, and here he was in the valley of the vineyards with a woman named Delilah. Her name means "to fade away; to become weaker, to decay or rot." Wow! Samson has really veered from the path of righteousness! Sin was about to lull Samson to sleep and make him its prisoner.

I want to make something clear here: "Delilah" doesn't have to be a man or a woman. It's the sin we fall in love with. We go through the five stages of sin, just as Samson did in falling in love with Delilah, and she sapped all the strength of God—all the anointing—away from him. She brought nothing but destruction into his life.

> *Delilah lulled Samson to sleep with his* *head in her lap, and she called in a man* *to shave off his hair, making his capture* *certain.* <u>And his strength</u> [the presence, the power of God] <u>left him.</u> *Then she cried out, "Samson! The Philistines have come to capture you!" When he woke up, he thought, "I will do as before and shake myself free." But he didn't realize the Lord had left him. So the Philistines captured him and gouged out his eyes. They took him to Gaza, where he was bound with bronze chains and made to grind grain in the prison.*
>
> —Judges 16:19-21 NLT (emphasis mine)

Samson played with sin a long time before he lost his anointing. And you and I can toy with sin a long time, and it can seem like we're getting away with it. But eventually it comes to the subjugation stage and literally lulls us to sleep. Samson having his eyes gouged out and being placed into chains is very symbolic. Practicing sin will bring us to a place of bondage and cause us to be spiritually blinded. The New Testament verses from 1 John bring this all home:

> *Anyone who loves other Christians is living in the light and does not cause anyone to stumble. Anyone who hates a Christian brother or sister* **is living and walking in darkness.** *Such a person is lost, having been blinded by the darkness.*
> —1 John 2:10-11 NLT (emphasis mine)

Walking out of love is a sin, and any sin that you and I practice causes us to walk in spiritual blindness. Spiritual blindness leads to bad decisions and dumb mistakes. We go down the wrong road instead of the right one and literally destroy our lives because of it. That's why God made sure we had the symbolism of the Bible story of Samson falling without repenting, continuing through the five stages of sin until he was in chains. Then God gave him yet another opportunity to repent as he was released from those chains, but he plunged deeper into sin until God had to allow the natural course of events to take place. Samson became his own worst enemy. He was lost to the point of physical blindness because he gave in to that first tiny temptation.

Many Christians, like Samson, become prisoners of their own decisions to sin and refuse to make it right with God. Ultimately, everything in their lives is destroyed. The devil's number-one goal concerning us is to keep us out of heaven so we can spend eternity in hell, because he wants everybody to be there with him. But once we accept Christ, Satan's next mission is to make sure we become an unproductive Christian who doesn't fulfill God's call and purpose on our lives. God's heart is just the opposite. He wants us to be holy, seated together with Him in heavenly places, living above sin and walking free from its destructive effects.

> God wants us to be holy, seated together with Him in heavenly places, living above sin and walking free from its destructive effects.

Samson repented and God restored his strength to him. He died when he knocked down the pillars in the sporting arena where he was chained. I believe his death is symbolic to us of dying to self and operating in the three principles that can set us free from sin! When it comes to the sin nature that all Christians have in their bodies, it's important to realize that it can be shut off! You'll never defeat it in a head-on battle, but you can shut it down or off! Note the powerful declaration in this scripture from Romans 6:

> *This we know—that our old self was nailed to the cross with Him, in order that* **our sinful nature** <u>*might be*</u> **deprived of its power,** *so that we should no longer be the slaves of sin.*
>
> —Romans 6:6
> Weymouth New Testament
> (emphasis mine)

We can deprive our sin nature of its power! If we do, we no longer have to be slaves to sin. It becomes our slave! Imagine a lamp plugged into a power source. The power source gives the lamp the juice it needs to light the bulb. If I were to pull the cord from the power source, you could flip the switch all day, but that lamp would not come on. When we learn to deprive our sin nature of its power—pull the cord out of our sin nature that lives in our bodies—no matter how often the devil flicks your switch with temptation, it's not going to respond. You'll be able to look at temptation and say, "I'm not going to fall for this. I rebuke you in the name of Jesus." You can walk away from it and live free. I'll show you how to deprive your sin nature of power.

Unfortunately, when temptation comes, most Christians often hold on for dear life hoping to beat that thing. God is saying, "No, no, no, no! Don't do that, pull the power cord out of your sin nature so you can resist that sin and walk away from it." These two scriptures show us how to do this:

> But <u>put on the Lord Jesus Christ</u>, **and make no provision for the flesh, to fulfill its lusts.**
> —Romans 13:14 NKJV (emphasis mine)

> I say then: <u>Walk in the Spirit,</u> and **you shall not fulfill the lust of the flesh.**
> —Galatians 5:16 KJV (emphasis mine)

The word *flesh* in both of these verses refers to our sin nature that lives in our bodies. It's referring to us yielding to it and sinning. Notice in both of these verses that you and I can avoid sinning by doing something positive! If we put on Christ or walk in the Spirit, we won't sin! Notice how a positive action shuts down our sin nature! How cool is that! We spend most of our time emphasizing the negative and trying not to do it, and the Bible simply says to put the positive into motion and you won't do the negative! You'll be strong enough to say no to sin!

Let's begin to talk about how to neutralize our sin nature by releasing these powerful principles! It was a journey for me to discover these truths. Before I accepted Christ at nineteen years of age, I struggled with sexual sin because of my brothers' *Playboy* magazines. I've mentioned this earlier, but it bears repeating. I was ten or eleven years old, and I found those magazines in the basement, hidden from my mom and dad. I never told anybody, but I went back every couple of days and looked at those magazines, and then they'd bring new books, and I'd look through all of them. It really affects you when you begin to see those images at a very young age. The moment I got saved, I knew I shouldn't be doing this, but the struggle didn't just evaporate. It was still very much there! After about a six-month honeymoon with Jesus, I started to fall back into sexual sin. I quickly returned to the synchronized stage of sin, serving God and practicing sin in harmony, and didn't understand how to get out of it! I wanted to really badly!

There were times when I would go to God crying and tell Him I was sorry. I came to believe that I had said I was sorry and repented so many times that I wondered if God even listened to me anymore. It went on and on. I probably repented fifty times in fifty days. "Oh, God, I'm so sorry," I would cry. I became so frustrated, I could hardly stand it. I looked for books and tapes to help me with this, but I couldn't find anything at the time. I really didn't even know where to look. Although I was going to a great church, they just weren't teaching practical things like this.

I remember making a decision to figure this out for myself. I just began to study the Bible. I didn't realize that God had called me to be a pastor or that He had given me a teaching gift at that time. But it was really easy for me to study, so I just started studying and figured it out for myself. I learned some things that I began to apply in my life that absolutely brought me to a place where I could conquer those particular things I'd been dealing with. None of us will ever be perfect in the sense that we won't make mistakes, but we can—yes, it is possible—to get to a place where we're not committing major sin in our lives and strong enough to say no to temptations.

> None of us will ever be perfect in the sense that we won't make mistakes, but we can say no to temptation.

There are days when I say things I shouldn't say, and I have to repent. There are days when I'm in a bad mood, grouchy, and want to bite somebody's head off. That has happened at home a few times. What do I have to do? I have to ask for that person's forgiveness as well as God's. We will never be perfect as long as we're living in this world, but we can overcome all kinds of sins through Jesus Christ. I have discovered three simple principles that will help anyone overcome sexual sin or any kind of sin whatsoever. I call them the ABCs of walking free from sin. The "A" stands for "Avoid triggers." "B" stands for "Be on guard." "C" stands for "Clothe yourself with God."

If you learn to avoid triggers, be on guard, and clothe yourself with God, you'll overcome every major sin you've ever struggled with, including homosexuality, pornography, sexual addictions, etc. Temptations might come, but if you learn the ABCs of walking free from sin and put them into practice, you'll be able to speak to temptation and command it to leave, as Jesus did, and it will. The first two principles are so important to follow, but it's the third one that will change everything! Yet you'll sabotage the third principle if you don't practice the first two. Let's talk about the first principle.

A. Avoid triggers.

A *trigger* is defined as "an event that precipitates other events,"[2] according to the dictionary. It refers to something that we come in contact with that is too strong for us to overcome. Obviously, we need to avoid certain things that will cause us to fall back into old patterns that were destructive and pulled us away from our relationship with the Lord. There are some atmospheres and situations that a Christian is not strong enough to enter! They will sin if they do—that's a trigger!

Jesus addressed this in His Word:

> *"So if your eye—even if it is your good eye—causes you to lust, **gouge it out and throw it away.** It is better for you to lose one part of your body than for your whole body to be thrown into hell. And if your hand— even if it is your stronger hand—causes you to sin, **cut it off and throw it away.** It is better for you to lose one part of your body than for your whole body to be thrown into hell."*
> —Matthew 5:29-30 NLT (emphasis mine)

These are some serious instructions! So let me ask you a question: Would it hurt to gouge out your eye? Would it hurt to cut off your hand? It would, believe me. I've never done it, but I know it would hurt. Now, Jesus was not saying that you and I literally have to gouge out an eye or have to cut off a hand. He is dealing with triggers! If something you do causes you to sin, stop doing it. The hand and eye are referring to the atmospheres we allow ourselves to go into. Sometimes we're not strong enough to handle certain atmospheres and must simply avoid them.

As a pastor, I counseled people a lot in the early days. Couples that were dating would come in to see me with tears in their eyes. "Pastor, we need your help. We want to tell you we're sorry, but we keep going too far," they said. "We know we shouldn't have sex until we're married, but we keep messing up." They were very sincere. They wanted to be free. I asked them questions and probed a little bit, "How is this happening?" I asked. "When is it happening?"

"Well, uh, you know, we're over at my apartment sitting on the couch, and we start to kiss," one or both would respond. "And every time we start to kiss, it just goes a little bit too far." You can't say it's a sin to kiss, because it isn't. But if kissing heats you up to a place where you can't stop, then it's a trigger. Some dating couples can be alone in a house and be okay. Others may not be able to be alone anywhere because they have a hunger for sex. Sorry for the strong words, but it's true! Some may be able to be alone, but if they sit on the couch and begin to kiss, they can't stop. So being alone or kissing can be a trigger, and is, for most dating couples. To avoid triggers, I very sweetly say: "Stay off the couch!"

I heard a very prominent pastor say something that had to do with triggers when I was in Bible school. He pastored a mega-church and was, in my opinion, very spiritual. He made a statement that absolutely made my jaw drop. I was stunned. Off course, my Bible knowledge and life experience could have fit inside a peanut at the time.

He said that he had a problem with girls and that he always had at least one guy with him and sometimes two when he traveled. He did this to insure that he would never be alone and vulnerable to sin.

He said, "I always make sure that one guy stays in my room with me. Why? Because I don't trust myself alone in a hotel room." I thought, *Wow, here's an exceptionally successful pastor who is admitting publicly that he has this weak spot, an eye that needs gouged out!* He was living holy at the time, but realized this was a huge area of temptation for him. He took the necessary steps to avoid the trigger of being alone.

It's no different for an alcoholic who hasn't had a drink in ten years making sure he doesn't walk into a liquor store or a bar. Why? Because the atmosphere will probably be more than he can handle.

I remember when I was first born again. I was watching "Gilligan's Island" one day on TV, and every time Mary Ann or Ginger came on, I would have these crazy sexual thoughts hit me. Before I met Jesus as Savior, the thoughts were there and I enjoyed them. I wasn't bothered by them at all. I knew they were wrong, but I couldn't get them out of my mind. Can you believe this innocent show was a trigger for me that caused me to sin?

I'd pray, go to church, and read my Bible, but every time I saw this show I was hit by those thoughts, and

I wasn't strong enough to ignore them. God dealt with me, before I knew what I'm teaching you now, to stop watching the show. When I did, I was okay! Now that I've grown and matured, I can watch re-runs of "Gilligan's Island" and be fine! But then I was too weak, and God had to deal with me to cut it out of my life. What are you watching on TV? Could anything you're watching be a trigger that is making you stumble into sin?

If you struggle with pornography, you'll probably either have to get rid of your computer or put your home computer in a location where it's out in the open and loaded with filters that you can't change in order to stay free from this problem. If you work the three principles and don't avoid triggers, you'll probably fall back into sin. Can you think of any triggers in your life?

B. Be on guard.

> *Above all else, guard your heart, for it is the wellspring of life.*
>
> —Proverbs 4:23

According to what Jesus taught in the parable of the sower found in Mark 4, our hearts can produce a crop of God's Word or anything else we feed on. Whatever we feed on the most, which is done by what we watch and listen to, will grow in our spiritual hearts, which includes our minds, and it will control us. When the Bible says to guard your heart, it is saying to watch the atmospheres that you allow yourself into. Watch what you feed on. Watch what you watch on television; watch

The things that you "feed" on will grow in you.

out for that music you listen to on your iPod. Just watch what you are allowing to get inside you. We have to be the guard of our own heart. I can't guard your heart. You have to guard your heart. It's between you and God.

The things that you "feed" on will grow in you. And if something is growing in you, then you won't have the strength to resist temptation when it comes. So the secret is to be on guard and don't allow the wrong things to come in to you.

According to the *Boston Globe*, a study in Pediatrics found that "adolescents who are regularly exposed to sex in media are more likely to have sex at ages 14 to 16 than those who have minimal exposure. While 12-to-14-year-olds exposed to sex through the media were 2.2 times more likely to participate in early sexual activity than their peers who reported the lowest exposure to media."[3]

What these young people feed on fills them up and they end up not being able to say no! If what a young person feeds on affects them, can what adults feed on affect us? It would have to! That's why we're told to guard our hearts. Let's talk a little more about our kids. From their earliest years, children watch television shows and movies that present "sex appeal" as a quality that people need to develop to the fullest. Teenagers are at risk from this sort of mass-market encouragement. The sexual content in the media greatly affects young people's sexual activity and beliefs about sex. *Marketing Sex to Children,* a fact sheet from the Campaign for a Commercial Free Childhood, offers these statistics:

> ❱ In 2003, 83 percent of the episodes of the top 20 shows among teen viewers contained some sexual content, including 20 percent with sexual intercourse.

> ❱ 42 percent of the songs on the top CDs in 1999 contained sexual content—19 percent included direct descriptions of sexual intercourse.

> ❱ On average, music videos contain 93 sexual situations per hour, including eleven "hard core" scenes depicting behaviors such as intercourse and oral sex.

> ❱ Girls who watched more than 14 hours of rap music videos per week were more likely to have multiple sex partners and to be diagnosed with a sexually transmitted disease.[4]

Even secular studies tell us that what we feed on we end up doing. So we need to be on our guard.

The Bible also teaches that the company you keep—your closest friends—will either bring you up or bring you down.

> Do not be misled: "**Bad company corrupts good character.**" Come back to your senses as you ought, and stop sinning; for there are some who are ignorant of God—I say this to your shame.
> —1 Corinthians 15:33-34 (emphasis mine)

> Become wise by walking with the wise; **Hang out with fools and watch your life fall to pieces.**
> —Proverbs 13:20 THE MESSAGE
> (emphasis mine)

We cannot ignore the fact that those we are around most have the most influence on us. Why is that? Because what they say, what they talk about, what we do together is going to feed us. Let's face it—we become who we hang out with. When I was growing up, my parents had a saying that they always brought out when they weren't happy with a new friend we'd brought home: "Birds of a feather flock together." That was mom and dad's way of telling us they didn't approve of something about this new acquaintance. They might have been unable to say exactly what it was—an attitude, the way they talked about things or about other people—but something just wasn't quite right. They didn't want our new friend's attitude to "rub off" on us.

At that time, my parents didn't understand the Bible or anything about God's opinion on the subject of who their kids associated with, but they understood that who you hang out with is who you become.

Who are your dearest and closest friends? This is important because they are affecting your life. Even if I had never met you, I could learn a lot about you just by getting to know your closest friends. I could tell you what is important to you, the goals that you are pursuing—what you hope to accomplish. The law of association simply refers to taking on the characteristics and traits of those you spend time with—becoming like them.

Good people can have great character, but if they begin to run with the wrong crowd, the Bible says their character will be corrupted. This is the negative side of the law of association. People can pull us down and change our character. But the positive side is that we can hang out with people who literally pull us up, not only in character but also in our spiritual walk. Now, I'm not saying that you can't spend time with someone who is a sinner. On the contrary—God wants us to be concerned about sinners and extend ourselves enough to let them know we care about them. But we must be cautious about who our closest friends are. What are your closest friends like? They're either taking you up or down.

It's important for me to take a minute to deal with you about spending some time with non-Christians. I think all Christians should reach out to people who are living in sin and don't know Christ.

> All Christians should reach out to people who are living in sin and don't know Christ.

We should have coffee with them and sit down with them at work and have lunch. That doesn't mean we're saying, "Let's party together." No. We do what is right—we talk with them and show that we care about them, but we also guard our hearts. When you are on guard, you're not opening up your heart to anything they are doing wrong. You are striving to reach out to them and bring them to Christ. That should be the heart of every Christian. We should invite people to church and small groups, and do everything we can do to connect them with God and help change their lives.

As Christians we must be careful that we don't have an elitist attitude that says we are holy and don't want anything to do with sinners. No. God expects us to help sinners by pulling them up to a higher spiritual level. It is important to think about who influences you most.

In thinking and praying about it, God may start dealing with you about changing some of your friends. He may show you that you're hanging with the wrong crowd—a crowd that is bringing you down. That is when you will have to prune some friends out of your life. It may be painful, but you can be sure that you will be better for it.

> *"If you want to be my follower **you must love me more** than your own father and mother, wife and children, brothers and sisters—yes, more than your own life. Otherwise, you cannot be my disciple. And you cannot be my disciple if you do not carry your own cross and follow me."*
> —Luke 14:26-27 NLT (emphasis mine)

These verses helped me to make some tough decisions at a time in my life when I really needed help. In order to be a true follower of Jesus, you must first decide whom you love the most because that is the person you will strive to please. Jesus requires that we love Him more than our closest relatives, because only then can we truly serve Him in a way that pleases Him. Making that decision may not be popular with all your relatives and friends, but that is a cross you'll have to bear. Notice that verse 27 says we must make a decision to carry our cross, which means we may suffer rejection and persecution. But obeying Christ is always best, and He will take care of the rest.

When my son David was in junior high, he hung out with all kinds of friends. Then, in high school, I began to notice that he was staying home every Friday night. Finally, I asked, "Dave, what are you doing at home? It's Friday night. Why aren't you hanging with your friends?" I'll never forget his answer. He looked at me teary eyed and said, "Dad, my friends are backslidden right now and not living for God. Some of them are partying and doing things they shouldn't do. I made a decision to go with God long ago, and if I am going to go with God, I can't hang with those friends—they will pull me down. So I decided just to stay home." Part of me felt broken because my son was hurting due to his friends, but another part of me was very proud of him. Completely on his own, he had decided to put his relationship with God first. And I watched God bless his life because of it. God flooded him with some really great and close friends, but he had to hurt for a while and carry a cross that was painful so he could grow and go on with God.

The wonderful thing is that by choosing to walk with people who are in love with Jesus, it will rub off on you. So you should always choose friends who have wisely chosen to walk with God. Who are you hanging out with? Who is your best friend?

When we're on our guard, we make sure our friends are going in the same direction we're going. If folks aren't going after God, we don't want them to take us down, so we might have to bring the "Avoid Triggers" principle in.

We may even have to cut off some relationships, as my son had to do, because the wrong relationships will feed us the wrong way and will really hurt us. So A, you avoid triggers; B, you have to be on guard. You have to watch what gets into you.

C. Clothe yourself with God.

We clothe ourselves with God in two ways. Let's talk about the first way. Just a few pages back, I referenced Romans 13:14 that admonishes us to "put on the Lord Jesus Christ." One way we *put on* the Lord is to feed on His Word. Colossians 3:16 instructs us to "let the word of Christ dwell in you richly." There are two key words here, *let* and *richly.* God says it's our responsibility to allow His Word to dwell in us richly. We have to decide how much of His Word we want. It's up to us how we respond to His direction to fill ourselves up with His Word.

> *The Word of God is living and active.*
> *Sharper than any double-edged sword, it*
> *penetrates even to dividing soul and spirit,*

joints and marrow; it judges the thoughts
and attitudes of the heart.
　　　　—Hebrews 4:12 (emphasis mine)

The Bible is unlike any other book. It can get inside of us, open itself up to us and reveal everything. It is filled with life. We clothe ourselves or put on Christ by filling ourselves up with the Word of God. As we read the Word and fill up on it, we flood or saturate our spirit, soul, and body with life. It pulls the plug or the cord out of our sin nature. We actually deprive our sin nature of power when we saturate ourselves with God's Word, the Bible. So when the devil tries to flip our switch with temptation, nothing happens. We can tell him to get lost in the name of Jesus. We have the power to resist him because we're feeding on the Word of God.

It also renews our mind and changes us from the inside out! The second way we cloth ourselves with God is by walking in the Spirit or saturating ourselves with the Spirit as we read earlier.

Be very careful, then, how you live—not
as unwise but as wise, making the most of
every opportunity, because the days are evil.
Therefore do not be foolish, but understand
what the Lord's will is. Do not get drunk on
wine, which leads to debauchery. **Instead,**

be filled with the Spirit. <u>Speak to one another with psalms, hymns and spiritual songs. Sing and make music in your heart to the Lord,</u> always giving thanks, to God the Father for everything, in the name of our Lord Jesus Christ.
　　—Ephesians 5:15-20 (emphasis mine)

When we get drunk on too much alcohol, it influences our life and our actions. In the same way, God wants us to fill ourselves with the Holy Spirit because that will influence our actions too. And when I see the phrase, "be filled with the Spirit," I think of the day I got saved. My Bible fell open to 1 Corinthians chapters 12, 13, and 14. I kept seeing the phrase *speaking with other tongues.* On that day, I was filled with the Holy Spirit and spoke with other tongues! I realize that some people don't believe in speaking in other tongues, and that is okay. You can still fill yourself with the Holy Spirit by doing the next verse of the section of this scripture from Ephesians. If you are a Spirit-filled believer, you realize that being filled with the Spirit is something we do by praying in the Holy Spirit.

> Holy Spirit prayer releases the life of the Holy Spirit in us and fills and floods us with God's own Spirit.

Although praying in the Holy Spirit (tongues) can be employed in intercessory prayer, it isn't for that purpose alone. Holy Spirit prayer releases the life of the Holy Spirit in us and fills and floods us with God's own Spirit. If you've ever prayed in the Spirit, you know when you are finished praying that you feel different. Why? Because you've flooded yourself with the life of God. Every time we pray in the Spirit, we're pulling the power plug out of the sin nature that lives in our bodies.

We can also walk in the Spirit or be filled with the Spirit by praising and worshiping God! The Bible teaches us that when we praise God, He inhabits our praises. That's what Ephesians means when it says to "speak to one another in psalms, hymns, and spiritual songs. Sing and make music in your heart to the Lord." We're literally inviting God to come down and dwell with us when we're praising Him. It brings us into the very presence of God. That's life—Holy Spirit life.

Years ago I made a decision to saturate myself with God. I realized that if I did this I would not fulfill the lusts of my sin nature. I could live holy. I'd have the strength to overcome temptation every time it came at me. I think it's so important that Christians read their Bible every day. I have one of those "One Year" Bibles, and I read the designated section of the day first thing in the morning every single day.

Further, I love to meditate on scriptures. I grab one scripture a week and think about it all day long. I'm saturating myself with the life of God when I do this. It takes about ten to twelve minutes to read my Bible and pick out my verse that I meditate on, and even in the shower, I just think about that verse. I recall it at different times during the day. When I lay down to sleep, I think about it. It keeps my mind clean and holy.

Worship is another way to saturate yourself with God. Every morning of my life, I sing along with the songs on my favorite worship CDs. I lock the door to my office, turn off the light, and play that music so loud it shakes my body. I just sing with all my heart and see myself as if I'm right before the throne of God. I worship God from my heart. It takes me into His presence, and I know that if I hang out in the presence of God, it's going to saturate me. I know it's going to pull the power cord out of my sin nature, and I'm going to have a good day. I have become a worship-holic because I want to help God explode life inside of me. Each of us needs to put on Christ and walk in the Spirit. This is how we clothe ourselves with God! These are the key principles that pull the power cord out of our sin nature!

There's nothing like going through life free from the bondage of sin. It is so wonderful to be in a position to say no to the enemy when he tempts me, and he does.

He'll never quit. But he has no power over me because I have clothed myself in the Spirit.

How do we make no provision for the flesh to fulfill its lusts? We put on the Lord Jesus Christ and then we automatically make no provision for our flesh. If you walk in the Spirit, you won't fulfill the lust of the flesh. Walking in the Spirit and putting on the Lord Jesus Christ, that's what I mean when I say clothe yourself with God. So avoid triggers, be on guard, and clothe yourself with God if you want to walk free from sin and fill yourself with as much of God as you can.

If you are feeding on the Bible, you are clothing yourself with God.

At the church I pastor in Ohio, we teach the importance of making sure that those who attend our church are regularly reading the Bible. Why? Because if you are feeding on the Bible, you are clothing yourself with God. We urge the members of our church in Ohio to listen to good, wholesome music. I love to listen to praise and worship music, and as you listen to praise and worship music, again, you are clothing yourself with God and filling spirit, soul, and body with good things. So you're on your guard watching what gets in there, but you're making sure that good things are being flooded into you. And the more of the good things you spend time with, the better off you'll be.

Reading your Bible and good books, listening to some good CDs like "Pastor Joe" CDs and great praise and worship music like the music CDs from our church—clothing yourself with God—is transforming. You are able to speak to any issue [challenge, temptation] and say, "I'm not going to give you a place in my life." You're able to walk away from it before it can draw you into it. What happened? The ABCs of walking free from sin—avoiding triggers, being on guard, and clothing yourself with God—have been activated in your life.

I can guarantee you that as a Christian, if you begin to bring these ABCs into your life, you'll grow into a higher place of walking as a friend of God and having an intimate relationship with Him. The joy is in the journey. Now is the time. Why not get started today?

God's Opinion in Review
Chapter 10

▌ Many lives are being destroyed on a daily basis by addiction to pornography. In fact, surveys indicate that 37 percent of pastors said pornography was a struggle for them and 51 percent admitted it was a temptation.

▌ Christians who aren't applying biblical principles to their lives struggle with sin in exactly the same way as non-Christians. Although their sin stain has been removed from their spirit, it still lives in their bodies.

▌ An excellent example of the destructive effects of sin is found in the story of the Old Testament Nazirite, Samson, from Judges 13-16. Like many of us, even Samson, separated from birth to devote his life to God and holiness, struggled with the five stages of sin: (1) Seduction stage; (2) Satisfaction stage; (3) Synchronization stage; (4) Shamelessness stage; (5) Subjugation stage.

▌ The Nazirite code included: (1) Could not cut hair; (2) Could not drink wine or other fermented drinks;

(3) Could not eat grapes or any product from the vine; (4) Could not go near a dead body (animal or human); (5) Could not eat anything unclean, i.e., pork or shellfish; (6) Required to obey the Mosaic Law.

∎ We can become so comfortable with sin that we become hardened in our conscience without even realizing that sin is hanging around in our lives.

∎ When Christians learn to walk holy and conquer sin, we won't find sin acceptable in ourselves or others. We will come to abhor sin as God abhors sin—not the sinner but the sin. The world we live in won't know what to do with us because we'll look and act so differently as we love sinners and help them to resist sin.

∎ God is creating many Phinehases in this age—people who have the spirit of holiness on them and find it vitally important to live a holy and clean life.

∎ We can fall in love with sin just as Samson fell for Delilah, but it will sap the strength and anointing of God from our lives and bring nothing but destruction.

∎ Most of us will never be perfect in the sense that we won't make mistakes, but we can get to a place where we are not committing major sin in our lives and are strong enough to say no to temptation.

▮ The ABCs of walking free from sin: (A) Avoid triggers. (B) Be on guard. (C) Clothe yourself with God.

▮ The Bible, unlike any other book, can get on the inside of us, open itself up to us and reveal everything we need to know about living a holy and pure life. It renews our mind and changes the way we think and look at life. We are saturated with the Holy Spirit and come to know God in an entirely new dimension.

▮ Praying in other tongues releases the life of the Holy Spirit in us and fills and floods us with God's own Spirit.

▮ Our praise to God causes Him to inhabit our praises. It ushers the very presence of God into our lives. Listen to good music and "Pastor Joe" teaching CDs. Read good books in addition to reading your Bible every single day of your life. Saturate yourself with Christ, and you will be able to resist temptation.

Turn or Burn Mentality?

N MY OPINION, MANY CHRISTIANS WHO love and serve Jesus come across in a condescending way with unbelievers who don't practice what the Bible says. So many Christians come off, probably without realizing it sometimes, with a "turn or burn" mentality. While the Bible does preach against practicing sin and does list what is sin and what's not sin, we Christians have to understand the context in which God is saying these things.

When God's people—such as the Jews in the Old Testament or Christians in the New Testament—are practicing sin, there is a bit of a "turn or burn" attitude coming out of God. Remember, He's talking to His people who acknowledge Him and believe the Bible is His word to mankind. Yet the Bible deals totally differently with people who aren't confessing Christians. We should do the same. We don't compromise the Bible or our standards. We simply understand who we're communicating with.

Let's face it, according to what we discovered already in a previous chapter, anyone—good or bad—who does not accept Jesus cannot enter heaven's gates. Their only alternative is hell. So our goal isn't to clean people up on the outside first, but on the inside first, by bringing them to Christ. Our goal is to preach Christ to them. I believe God will convict them of their sins. We need to preach Christ and simply tell them that all have sinned, He came to save sinners, and He'll save them!

The one message God wants us to share with unbelievers is simply that we all need Christ. If we don't accept Him, we are going to have problems. The little grandma who crochets doilies, makes cookies for her grandkids, and is really a nice person—but not a born again Christian—is going to go to the same hell as a practicing homosexual who is not born again.

Remember that all of us have sinned and fallen short of the glory of God. We have a sin problem by birth. I've coined a phrase that I kind of like because it gets the message across. It's really simple but it's this phrase: "Dogs bark, cats meow, birds tweet, and sinners sin." I've never heard a cat bark. I've never heard a bird meow, I've never heard a dog sing, "tweet, tweet," and I never will because dogs bark, cats meow, birds tweet, and sinners sin. So we have to come to a place where we realize that unsaved people are going to do what they do.

> We shouldn't be shocked by what the world does. There is only one solution for this world—it's Jesus.

We shouldn't be shocked by what the world does. There is only one solution for this world—it's Jesus. It is Jesus and Him only who will change the world and provide the strength to live right. God wants us to set a standard without being judgmental, He wants us to live it and let them see it! I'm very careful not to preach dos and don'ts to non-Christians. I simply aim to share Christ with them, knowing that He will clean them up once they accept Him.

Jesus himself followed these very principles. In the eyes of the religious people of His day, Jesus was a radical. Notice how He operated:

> *As Jesus went on from there, he saw a man named Matthew sitting at the tax collector's booth. "Follow me," he told him, and Matthew got up and followed him. While Jesus was having dinner at Matthew's house, **many tax collectors and "sinners"***

came and ate with him and his disciples.
<u>*When the Pharisees saw this, they asked*</u>
<u>*his disciples,*</u> **"Why does your teacher eat**
with tax collectors and 'sinners'?" *On*
hearing this, Jesus said, "It is not the healthy
who need a doctor, but the sick. But go and
learn what this means: 'I desire mercy, not
sacrifice.' For I have not come to call the
righteous, but sinners."

—Matthew 9:9-13 (emphasis mine)

What a powerful text! First of all tax collectors were considered the worst sinners of the day because they were Jews who worked for the Roman government collecting taxes from their fellow Jews. That made tax payers mad to begin with, but then the tax collectors took extra money for themselves. If Rome wanted 10 percent, they took 20 percent, and kept 10 percent for themselves. So these guys were super wealthy at the expense of their fellow Jews. They were considered the worst of sinners, and here was Jesus eating and fellowshipping with them. The religious leaders saw it and got mad. How could He do this? What was wrong with Jesus? Well, Jesus wasn't sitting there smoking a cigar and getting drunk and telling dirty jokes. He was there on a mission. He was there to tell them about salvation.

He was setting an example for His followers and the religious people of the day, showing them that their mission was to go out and bring in the sinners. It was a demonstration that the purpose of His mission on earth—and their mission as well—was to share Christ with them. Jesus didn't want them to build walls around themselves to keep the sinners out. He wanted them to go after them and love them. Jesus said, "Guys, figure this out—I desire mercy not sacrifices." He was speaking to religious people who knew the Bible, the Law of Moses, and the sacrifices He referred to here were the tithes and the offering of animal sacrifices. Jesus said, "I'd rather have you be a person of mercy above all those things."

I am not pointing any of these things out as if I were never a sinner. I was a sinner, but God set me free, and He wants to set other people free too. When I was in Bible school, I strived to follow Jesus' example. I used to enjoy street witnessing, so I took a couple of buddies one Friday night and we went to downtown Tulsa. At the time, that was not a particularly safe neighborhood to be in. We were looking for people to share Jesus with.

We walked by a house where three prostitutes stood on the porch doing what they do, and they called us to come on over. I didn't think about shouting out, "Repent or burn!" Why? They were simply trapped in sin and needed to meet Jesus so He could set them free. So I asked my friends to join me and go witness to them. They said, "No way. If somebody from Bible school sees us, we'll be kicked out of school." I said, "If someone from Bible school's down here, they're not going to say anything about it." I was sure we were safe and said, "Now, guys, let's go." So we went. I got up on the porch, and the girls invited me to come inside. I declined, saying that I just wanted to talk to them.

They asked what I wanted to talk about. So I told them, "I'd like to talk to you about your salvation, your eternity, where you're going to go when you die." They said, "We're prostitutes. God doesn't like us. God doesn't love us. I said, "Well, that's not true. All of us have sinned. We have all done things wrong, but God wants to set us all free through Jesus Christ." I shared Christ with them, and after ten minutes or so, they said, "Yes, we'll pray with you." So the three prostitutes, my friends, and I joined hands and prayed. Those ladies accepted Christ as their Savior. Isn't God cool? They knew that what they were doing was wrong. They just needed a Christian who wouldn't condemn them to share the Good News!

I invited them to come to church on the following Sunday. I gave them my phone number and said I

> The three prostitutes, my friends, and I joined hands and prayed. Those ladies accepted Christ as their Savior.

would have some girls and a couple of guys come down and pick them up. They picked them up and brought them to church, and those girls were so excited to be at church. It was such a joy to see. A couple of weeks later, one of their pimps called me. This guy said, "Are you Joe Cameneti?" I said, "Yes." He said, "I'm going to kill you." Now, I got nervous, and when I'm nervous I joke around. I asked him, "Why do you want to kill me? I wouldn't be fun to kill! I think you have the wrong guy!"

He said, "Well, my girls aren't working anymore. They're going to church, and you have taken away my income." I explained that I had only shared Christ with the girls, and that it was God who was cleaning up their lives. Then I asked where he was with God and began to witness to him. "I don't want to hear this stuff," he said. I invited him to have coffee with me sometime so we could talk. "Just leave my girls alone!" he said and hung up on me. He didn't kill me—I'm still here and very much alive. But those girls grew in the Lord, and they changed. I didn't preach to them about the sin of being a prostitute—that was obvious. I preached Christ to them, and they responded to His love. This is the best way that I know of to deal with sinners God's way. God loves the sinner. He just hates the sin.

We aren't to condemn the non-Christians, but we also can't compromise our stance. I don't try to force my beliefs concerning what sin is and isn't down their throats, but I do have to teach Christians and anyone who asks what God's opinion is!

In today's world, there's a movement called the tolerance movement. They want us to say it's okay, it's not sin, but we can't do that. An extraordinarily gifted man named Mel White pastored West Coast churches for many years. In addition to pastoring churches, he was a talented ghostwriter for fellow evangelicals Jerry Falwell (*Strength for the Journey* and *If I Should Die Before I Wake*), Pat Robertson (*America's Date with Destiny*), Billy Graham (*Approaching Hoofbeats*), and several other Christian leaders. In 1994, White came out of the closet, announcing his homosexuality. He had been married since 1962 and was the father of two children. He embarked on a long process of attempted "cures" for his homosexuality, including psychotherapy, prayer, electroconvulsive therapy, and exorcism. None of these techniques changed his homosexuality, and after he attempted suicide, he and his wife agreed to an amicable divorce. May I say that my heart breaks for Mel at this stage in his life. I think my book could have helped him understand what he was dealing with.

"In 1984, White began dating Gary Nixon. As of 2007, they are still together, both as a couple and as leaders of the gay rights organization called Soulforce. In 1994, White wrote his autobiography, *Stranger at the Gate: To Be Gay and Christian in America,* which detailed his former career in the religious right and his struggle coming to terms with being gay. In 1997, White was awarded the ACLU's National Civil Liberties Award for his efforts to apply the soul force principles of Mahatma Gandhi and Martin Luther King Jr. to the struggle for justice for sexual minorities."[1]

White's Soulforce movement often organized picketing demonstrations at church meetings held by the late Jerry Falwell and other ministers. He also writes a lot of material against Christians teaching that homosexuality and other sexual lifestyles are sins. In an interview on the Internet by *The Intelligence Report,* Mel White was asked, "You don't believe the religious right truly loves the sinner but hates the sin?" Mel White replied, "To say 'I love you, but I have reservations' is to say, 'I don't love you.' To say 'I love you as you are,'—that's love. There is no 'but' or 'if' in love. When are they going to get that? You can't love the sinner and hate the sin when the sin is what I *am.* I am a gay man, and I love my partner of 23 years, Gary Nixon. Can you love me and not love my relationship with Gary? Give us a break! Quit using that. That is total false advertising. You don't love me at all unless you love me as I am."[2]

I truly love Mel—I simply don't agree with him. I want Mel to go to heaven just as you do, but I can't say that what Mel does is right. I can treat Mel with dignity and simply state what the Bible says, which he knows, and go on with my life and understand that only God can convince Mel. After studying the subject in the Bible, I'd have to say that the homosexual lifestyle is wrong. According to God, it is wrong, and if you practice something that God says is wrong, it's a sin.

> All of us have to deal with sin, and we must understand that if God said it's wrong, it is sin.

It's the same as having sex outside of marriage between a man and a woman—it is wrong. It's the same as stealing something—it is wrong. If somebody steals something and tells me, "Well, I'm a thief and that's what thieves do, so you have to love me," I would have to say, "No, stealing is wrong." All of us have to deal with sin, but we must understand that if God said it's wrong, it is sin.

I believe that we Christians need to live the life and be ready to share the Good News with anyone who wants to know. That's all, plain and simple. Now, when we're dealing with Christians who sin, it's a different standard that we are to go by. That's another book!

God's Opinion in Review
Chapter 11

▌ Many Christians appear to have a "turn or burn" mentality when it comes to dealing with unbelievers. While the Bible preaches against practicing sin and keeping company with those who do, we are to demonstrate the love of Christ to unbelievers and not be critical and judgmental.

▌ We need to preach Christ and simply tell unbelievers that He came to save sinners, that all have sinned, including all of us, and He saved us and can save them.

▌ It is Jesus and Him only who will change the world and provide the strength to live right.

▌ Jesus doesn't want us to build walls around ourselves to keep sinners out. He wants us to go after them and love them.

▌ Although we aren't to condemn non-Christians, we also cannot compromise our stance.

▌ A "tolerance" movement that saturates much of today's world wants us to say everything is okay and that nothing is really sin. It is not true. All of us have to deal with sin and we must understand that if God says something is wrong, it is sin.

Do You Hate Sin?

FOR EVERY CHRISTIAN THERE IS A level of growth in God that brings us to a place where sin is something we literally hate. As we place the ABCs principles of walking free from sin into motion, they not only shut down our flesh but they begin to renew our mind—the very way we think and look at life. The Bible teaches us that a Christian can come to a place in their spiritual life where they hate sin! That's right; you read that correctly. You and I can actually come to a place in our lives where we are not struggling to resist sin because we actually hate sin! Think about what it means to hate something.

I'll give you a very personal example to help bring this point home. When Gina and I were newlyweds, I was totally unaware that she hated mayonnaise. Of course, I love mayo. You can mess with me in many ways and not shake me up, but don't be messing around with my mayo! To me, a sandwich is not a sandwich without mayo on it.

So we were newly married and living in our first little rented house, and we were going to have lunch together one day. Gina was already sitting at the kitchen table, and I was at the counter making a sandwich. She wasn't paying much attention, but I was just plastering mayo on this sandwich—I mean it was coming out the sides. So I took my sandwich over to the table and sat down, ready to have a wonderful lunch with my wife of only a few weeks.

All of a sudden Gina came to life. It began with her sniffing and her reaction was amazing. When she discovered that I had mayo on my sandwich she went ballistic. First, she let out a blood-curdling scream, followed by, "Is that mayo? Is that mayonnaise? What are you doing with that mayo?"

"I'm going to eat it, Love," I said.

"Not in here you're not!" Gina proclaimed.

"What is the big deal?" I asked.

"I hate mayo! I can't take it," she said. "It makes me sick! I can't even take the smell, let alone eat it!" She went on to say, "You can't eat that in here. Go in the other room and eat it."

I could see that I wasn't going to win this battle, and as I started to go into the next room to eat my lunch, she screamed again, "You have to close the lid and put the jar away, now!"

"But it's ten feet away from you on the counter. Can't I do it later, after I eat?"

"No!" she said.

"Okay! Okay!" I said.

As I finally sat all alone in the other room, I wondered, *How did I marry a woman who doesn't like mayo? Life is cruel!* When it comes to hating something, I think this is a great example. When you hate something, you are appalled to be in its presence and want nothing to do with it at all! You will run in disgust from it and attempt to avoid it at all cost.

Is that how you feel about sin? Or is sin something that you tolerate, maybe even enjoy? Remember, we can come to a place where we actually hate sin. Let's take a look at what the Bible says we have to do in order to come to hate sin.

> *All who fear the* LORD **will hate evil.**
> —Proverbs 8:13 NLT (emphasis mine)

> *Through the fear of the* LORD ***a man avoids evil.***
> —Proverbs 16:6 (emphasis mine)

We see the key to hating evil, or sin, is to fear the Lord our God. We will take a look at what it means to fear the Lord in a moment. Think about what the scriptures are saying. When we fear the Lord, we go in a different direction just to stay away from sin. But that's not all. When we grow in the fear of the Lord, we come to a place where we literally hate sin—it is disgusting to us. This is the place I want to live in, how about you? A place where sin isn't enticing, but disgusting! Sin should have the same effect on us as mayo does on Gina!

All of us face various kinds of temptations. If you have ever channel-surfed your television, you know that there are a lot of crazy and sinful things on it. And one day when you least expect it, the devil will tempt you to watch one of those shows. Your eye will see something that you know is sinful, and you'll think, *Do I keep going or do I stop? That sure is enticing, but I know God doesn't want me to watch it. Hmmm. Maybe I'll watch a little bit of it and repent in the morning.* So you watch the show, feel terrible about it, tell the Lord how sorry you are that you did it, and ask Him to forgive you.

God wants us to be spiritually mature enough that we are disgusted rather than enticed by a sinful show.

That is how many Christians are with sin. They haven't yet become spiritually mature enough to hate sin to the extent that they find it disgusting and can't stand to be near it. God wants us to be spiritually mature enough that we are disgusted rather than enticed by a sinful show. When we see it, we can't get away from it quickly enough. It is exciting to live at that level and every one of us can do it. Let's begin to discover what it means to fear the Lord, because it's the key to hating sin!

> A wise man **fears the LORD** <u>and shuns evil</u>.
> —Proverbs 14:16 (emphasis mine)

It is important to understand what it means to *fear* God. Do you fear God the same way you fear a bully, an abusive boss, or an abusive spouse? To some Christians that is what it means to fear God, but is that what the Bible teaches us about the fear of the Lord? That reminds me of when I introduced my wife, Gina (then my fiancée), to my mom and dad. My dad is quite a tease, and as soon as I made the introduction, he gestured like he was going to give someone the backhand, and teasingly said, "Now, Joe, if you want to have a good marriage, you need to start this way and say, 'Woman, this is for nothing, so don't start nothing.'" Just when he said this he let his backhand go! Gina wasn't sure if he was joking or not at this time. I tried this system, but for some reason Gina wouldn't live under it. Yeah, right!

However, I believe some people fear God because they believe He is sitting up in heaven ready to smack them with a backhand every time they get out of line. Is that the fear of the Lord? Well, I'm excited to tell you that none of the above are the fear of the Lord! Yet there is a fear of the Lord and understanding it helps us hate and avoid sin! Let's talk about what it truly means to fear God.

> *For we* [Christians] <u>*must all*</u> **appear before the judgment seat of Christ,** *that each one may receive what is due him for the things done while in the body, whether good or bad.* **Since, then, we know what it is <u>to fear the Lord,</u>** *we try to persuade men."*
> —2 Corinthians 5:10-11 (emphasis mine)

Now all has been heard; here is the conclusion of the matter:

> **Fear God and keep his commandments,** *for this is the whole duty of man.*
> <u>*For God will bring*</u> **every deed into judgment, including every hidden thing, whether it is good or evil.**
> —Ecclesiastes 12:1-14 (emphasis mine)

Fearing God is connected to Judgment Day. Every Christian has to appear before the judgment seat of Christ to receive a judgment for the good and bad things we did while living on this earth. That's scary, isn't it? Paul calls the understanding of Judgment Day the fear of the Lord in 2 Corinthians. He says when you understand this judgment that you will actually persuade others to live correctly!

To fear the Lord is to have a conscious awareness that you and I will answer for everything we do while living on planet earth! Solomon also brings this same truth out in the book of Ecclesiastes. Our lifestyle changes when we realize that we have to answer for how we live our life down here on the earth.

Remember, when you fear the Lord you hate sin. How many Christians can jump in bed with sin, as if it were okay? How many Christians can flirt with sin and pet it on the head and think nothing of it? How many Christians can watch things on television that would make Jesus sick to His stomach, if He could be made sick, like mayo does to my wife? If you can do these types of things, you haven't had a revelation of Judgment Day that awaits all of us.

I'm going to pray for you that you grow in the fear of the Lord so you come to the place where you hate sin! Remember, growing to this place of fearing the Lord is a process. It begins with you practicing the ABCs of walking free from sin. There truly is a Judgment Day for all Christians—a day when Jesus will evaluate our lives. A day when Jesus will bless us with rewards for the good things we have done and hold us accountable for the bad things we did that we didn't repent and get rid of. Think about going through your day and being aware that you have to answer to God for the things you do that day. Would that change the way you live? I think it would.

Judgment Day, for the Christian, has to be looked at through the eyes of grace! We must understand it is there, but from the correct perspective. While it is a fact that we are accountable to God, there are two things you must understand. *One, any sin that you committed before you met Jesus was washed away and forgiven.* Bible forgiveness means that God literally wiped your slate clean—those sins are forever erased. God has forgotten them, and He'll never remember them again. It's as if you never committed them, so none of those will come up on Judgment Day. I'm so excited that my life before Christ is washed clean, and I won't be held accountable for the terrible things I did! I am sure you are equally excited. Now, as exciting as this is, the next part is even more exciting.

Two, the sins you've committed as you've walked with the Lord are forgiven the same way. When you truly regret what you've done and sincerely repent from your heart, He forgives you the same way He did when you first accepted Him.

> *If we confess our sins to him, **he is faithful and just to forgive us and to cleanse us from every wrong.***
>   —1 John 1:9 NLT (emphasis mine)

This verse is written to Christians. When we repent of sins we commit and tell God we were wrong and ask him to forgive us, He does! None of the confessed and forgiven sins will be mentioned at the Judgment Seat of Christ. Think about it—that's pretty exciting.

We are saved by grace, not by works. If we knew we were going to be held accountable for every sin we've committed since we've been Christians, we'd probably give up. I know I would! But to know that those sins are forever vanished is cause for rejoicing, and should encourage us to live pure lives and be ready to meet the Lord.

To know that those sins are forever vanished is cause for rejoicing, and should encourage us to live pure lives.

We don't know when Jesus will come and catch us away to be with Him, but it could happen at any moment. One thing we do know is that any of us could leave this earth unexpectedly. We have no guarantee that we'll live to a ripe old age—or even that we'll live to see tomorrow, and how tragic it would be to leave this world with unresolved sin in our lives. And if we aren't ready when the time comes, whether it is Jesus coming back or us leaving early, we are going to have to answer for sin we didn't repent of. I believe we will go to heaven, but we will not have a good Judgment Day! I truly believe some Christians place so much emphasis on God's grace that they have no fear of God and live sloppy, sinful lives because of it. Part of fearing the Lord is living with the awareness that we have to answer to God for how we live our lives. So if we mess up, we repent quickly, make things right, and stay in fellowship with God because we know we will have to answer to our Maker.

In this book we have come to understand God's opinion on today's hottest sex topics. We have discovered how to walk above sexual sin, and now we understand that we can even grow to hate sin! Yeah! Think about growing to the place where pornography on the Internet, television, advertisements and magazines that feature inappropriate sexual content will truly disgust us. We will still love the one trapped in sin, but we will not be able to enjoy it or be near it!

I trust that your life will never be the same! Go forth and live a holy and pure life as you serve God!

God's Opinion in Review
Chapter 12

❚ The Bible teaches that a Christian can come to a place in their spiritual life where they actually hate sin—are repulsed by it to the extent that they flee from it.

❚ Proverbs says that all who fear the Lord will hate evil, and it is through our godly fear and reverence of the Lord that we avoid evil.

❚ Many Christians have grown comfortable with some sin. They haven't yet developed enough spiritually to hate sin to the point of being disgusted by it. God wants us to be spiritually mature enough that we are disgusted rather than enticed by a sinful show.

❚ It is important to understand what the fear of God really means. Fearing God is connected to Judgment Day. To fear the Lord is to have a conscious aware-ness that we will answer for every unrepented sin while we were living on planet earth.

❚ Our lifestyles change when we realize that we have to answer for how we live our lives down here on earth. The good news is that the sins of a Christian are looked at through the eyes of God's amazing grace. When we truly regret what we've done and have sincerely repented from our heart, God forgives us in the same way He did when we first accepted Him as our Lord and Savior.

▌ First John 1:9 tells us that God is faithful and just to forgive and cleanse us from every wrong if we confess our sins to Him. How tragic it would be to leave this world with unresolved sin in our lives! We aren't going to have a good Judgment Day, even though we will qualify for heaven, if unresolved sin has not been dealt with before God. We must repent and repent quickly after we knowingly sin.

▌ As we turn our backs on sin, we must remember to continue to love the sinner who is still in bondage to it. It is love and love only that will bring them to repentance.

Chapter 1

1. Paul Taylor, Cary Funk, Peyton Craighill, "Are We Happy Yet?" *Pew Research Center Publications,* February 13, 2006, http://pewresearch.org/pubs/?PubID=301.

2. George Barna, "Morality Continues to Decay," *The Barna Group: The Barna Update,* November 3, 2003, http://www.barna.org/FlexPage.aspx?Page=BarnaUpdate&BarnaUpdateID=152.

3. Ibid.

4. Ibid.

Chapter 2

1. William Harms, "Results of Sex Study by University Researchers Revealed in Two Books," *The University of Chicago Chronicle* 14, no. 4 (October 13, 1994), http://chronicle.uchicago.edu/941013/sex.shtml.

2. Ibid.

3. Ibid.

4. Ibid.

5. Glenn T. Stanton, "Why Marriage Matters: Article Overview," http://www.family.org/socialissues/A000000440.cfm.

6. Ibid.

7. Anne Morse, "The Best Sex," 1998, http://www.troubledwith.com/LoveandSex/A000000350.cfm?print=true&topic=love%20and.

8. Ibid.

9. Ibid.

Chapter 3

1. Lauren Winner, "3 Fibs and a Truth About Sex," *Leadership Journal,* April 1, 2005, http://ctlibrary.com/33328.

2. Centers for Disease Control, "Youth Risk Behavior Surveillance-United States, 2005," *Morbidity & Mortality Weekly Report 2006* 55 (SS-5):1-108, http://www.cdc.gov/HealthyYouth/sexualbehaviors/.

3. Alan Guttmacher Institute (AGI), "In Brief: Facts on American Teens' Sexual and Reproductive Health," New York: AGI, 2002. http://www.guttmacher.org/pubs/fb_ATSRH.html.

4. "New Book Offers Analysis of Sexual Behavior," *The University of Chicago Chronicle* 20, no. 9, February 1, 2001, http://chronicle.uchicago.edu/010201/sex-book.shtml.

5. Elizabeth Querna, "Most Teens Say Oral Sex Is Safe," *U.S. News and World Report,* April 4, 2005, http://www. usnews.com/usnews/health/briefs/sex/hb050404a.htm.

6. Charles Swindoll, *Sanctity of Life,* Insight for Living, September, 1998.

7. James Strong, *A Concise Dictionary of the Words in the Greek Testament; with Their Renderings in the Authorized English Version* (Nashville: Thomas Nelson, 1984), s.v. "porneia" (#4202), 59.

8. Mike Genung, "How Many Porn Addicts are in Your Church?" http://www.crosswalk.com/1336107/.

9. John Van Epp, PhD, *How to Avoid Marrying a Jerk,* (New York, New York: McGraw Hill, 2007), 299.

10. Centers for Disease Control, "Trends in Reportable Sexually Transmitted Diseases in the United States, 2005," *Sexually Transmitted Disease Surveillance 2005,* www.cdc. gov/std/stats/trends2005.htm.

11. Ibid.

12. Jerry Gramckow, "Why Sexual Purity Matters: Good Reasons for Sexual Purity," *Focus on the Family,* (accessed April 25, 2007) http://www.focusonthefamily.com/ focusagazine/publicpolicy/A000000195.cfm.

13. "NBA Iron Man A.C. Green is MARRIED!" May 1, 2002, http://clubac.com/whazhappenn/default. asp?DocumentID=202 (also DocumentID=215).

Chapter 4

1. Proven Men Ministries, "Pornography Statistics: Pornography/Sexual Immorality Within the Church," taken from *Christianity Today,* March 5, 2001, pp. 44-45, http://www.1wayout.org/pages/PrintStatistics.aspx.

2. Proven Men Ministries, "Pornography Statistics: Pornography/Sexual Immorality Within the Church," http://www.1wayout.org/pages/PrintStatistics.aspx.

3. Steve Arterburn, *Every Man's Battle* (Colorado Springs, CO: WaterBrook Press, 2000).

4. Family Safe Media, "Preserving Family Values in a Media Driven Society: Pornographic Statistics," http://www.familysafemedia.com/pornography_statistics.html.

5. Jan LaRue, "Road to Perversion Is Paved with Porn," April 27, 2006, citing Fiona Harvey, "Porn Sites Use Toy Brands to Attract Children," *London Financial Times,* November 16, 2000, p. 17, (accessed April 25, 2007) www.HumanEvents.com/Article.php?ID=14319.

Chapter 5

1. Jerry Gramckow, "Why Sexual Purity Matters: Good Reasons for Sexual Purity," *Focus on the Family* (accessed April 25, 2007), http://www.focusonthefamily.com/focusagazine/publicpolicy/A000000195.cfm.

2. Mary Warner, "60 Percent of Americans Think Sex Outside of Marriage Is Fine," *The Patriot News,* September 4, 2001, http://rense.com/general13/marr.htm.

3. Nathan Tabor, "America, Marriage, Values: Adultery Is Killing the American Family," *Canada Free Press,* September 23, 2005, http://www.canadafreepress.com/2005/tabor092305.htm.

4. Ibid. Author Nathan Tabor is a conservative political activist based in Kernersville, NC. He has his BA in psychology and his MA in public policy. This article appeared in the September 23, 2005, issue of *Canada Free Press* based in Toronto, Ontario.

5. Barnes & Noble.com-Books: *Affair!* By H. Cameron Barnes, Paperback/From the Publisher, http://search.barnesandnoble.com/booksearch/isbninquiry.asp?ean=9781581127775&z=y.

6. Barnes & Noble.com-Books: *50-Mile Rule* by Judith E. Brandt, Paperback/From the Publisher, http://search.barnesandnoble.com/booksearch/isbninquiry.asp?ean=9781580084147&z=y.

7. "DALLIANCES—'Miss Manners' of Adultery (interview with Judith E. Brandt)," *Chicago Tribune,* May 10, 2002, http://pqasb.pqarchiver.com/chicagotribune/access/118973910.html?dids=118973910:118973910&FMT=ABS&FMTS=ABS:FT&type=current&date=May+10,+2002&author=&pub=Chicago+Tribune&edition=&startpage=1&desc=DALLIANCES+.

8. Jane Weaver, "Lust, Love & Loyalty Survey: Many Cheat for a Thrill, More Stay True for Love: MSNBC.com/iVillage Survey Shows Fidelity Can Be a Tough Promise to Keep," *MSNBC,* April 16, 2007, http://www.msnbc.msn.com/id/17951664/.

9. Dr. Lana Staneli is quoted in a sermon outline entitled "Adultery" taken from http://www.christianhelps.org/adultery.htm. This was originally published in *NET News Now*, Washington, D.C., January 22, 1997.

10. Patrick F. Fagan and Robert E. Rector, "The Effects of Divorce on America," *The Heritage Foundation: Leadership for America*, June 5, 2000, http://www.heritage.org/Research/Family/BG1373.cfm.

11. David Popenoe, "Debunking Divorce Myths," *Discovery Health Channel*, 2002, http://health.discovery.com/centers/loverelationships/articles/divorce_print.html.

12. Americans for Divorce Reform, "Children of Divorce Getting Divorced Themselves; Becoming Teen Moms, Single Moms, Battered Wives," http://www.divorcereform.org/teenmoms.html, cited from Brian Willats, *Breaking Up is Easy to Do*.

13. Fagan and Rector, "The Effects of Divorce on America."

14. Rutgers University, "The State of Our Unions 2006," *The National Marriage Project, 2006*, http://marriage.rutgers.edu/Publications/SOOU/SOOU2006.pdf, cited from David Schramm, "Individual and Social Costs of Divorce in Utah," *Journal of Family and Economic Issues* 27 (2006):1.

Chapter 6

1. Joe Dallas, *When Homosexuality Hits Home: What to Do When a Loved One Says They're Gay* (Eugene, OR: Harvest House Publishers, 2004), 159.

2. William D. Mosher, Anjani Chandra, and Jo Jones, "Sexual Behavior and Selected Health Measures: Men and Women 15-44 Years of Age, United States, 2002," September 15, 2005, http://www.cdc.gov/nchs/products/pubs/pubd/ad/361-370/ad362.htm.

3. *Webster's II New College Dictionary*, s.v. "Abomination."

4. Ibid., s.v. "Detestable;" "Detest."

5. Ibid., s.v. "Perversion;" "Perverse."

Chapter 7

1. Simon LeVay, "A Difference in Hypothalmic Structure Between Heterosexual and Homosexual Men," *Carnegie Mellon School of Computer Science,* January 29, 1991, http://www.cs.cmu.edu/afs/cs.cmu.edu/user/scotts/bulgarians/nature-nurture/levay.html.

2. Warren Throckmorton, "New Genetics Study Undermines Gay Gene Theory," *UIC News Release*, February 9, 2005, http://www.drthrockmorton.com/id=128 cites a study by Brian S. Mustanski, et al., "A Genomewide Scan of Male Sexual Orientation," *Human Genetics,* 2005, http://mypage.iu.edu/~bmustans/Mustanski_etal_2005.pdf.

3. Exodus International, "What Causes Homosexuality?" © 2005 Exodus International, P.O. Box 540119, Orlando, FL 32854, by Dr. Joseph Nicolosi, http://exodus.to/content/view/504/186/.

4. Ibid.

5. Note what Alan Chambers of Exodus International [Global Alliance] says on page 137.

6. "Prominent Psychiatrist Announces New Study Results: 'Some Gays *Can* Change,'" *NARTH: National Association for Research & Therapy of Homosexuality*, May 9, 2001, http://www.narth.com/docs/spitzer2.html.

7. "Report Received from American Association of Christian Counselors," *American Association of Christian Counselors*, June 13, 2001, www.aacc.net/enews.html#enews_lead.

8. Exodus International, "Orlando Billboard Ads Feature Former Homosexuals: We Questioned Homosexuality: Truth Brought Freedom," April 12, 2005, http://exodus.to/content/view/293/37/.

Chapter 8

1. Alan Guttmacher Institute (AGI), "Get 'In the Know': 20 Questions About Pregnancy, Contraception and Abortion," cited from The Alan Guttmacher Institute (AGI), *Sharing Responsibility: Women, Society and Abortion Worldwide* (New York: AGI, 1999), Chart 1.1, http://guttmacher.org/in-the-know/index.html.

2. "Abortion in America: A Consumer-Behavior Perspective," *Journal of Consumer Research: An Interdisciplinary Quarterly, University of Chicago Press,* vol. 21(4), pages 677-94, March. Patterson, Maggie Jones & Hill, Ronald Paul & Maloy, Kate, 1995. http://ideas.repec.org/a/ucp/jconrs/v21y1995i4p677-94.html.

3. P. John Seward, MD, "American Medical Association [Letter to] The Honorable Rick Santorum," May 19, 1997, http://www.nrlc.org/abortion/pba/amaletter.html.

4. "Americans Divided on Abortion Rights," *Angus Reid Global Monitor: Polls & Research,* May 27, 2007, http://www.angus-reid.com/polls/index.cfm/fuseaction/viewItem/itemID/15880.

5. *Wikipedia,* s.v. "Abortion: Public Opinion," http://en.wikipedia.org/wiki/Abortion#Public_opinion.

6. "Teens in Trouble Statistics," *Battle Cry Newsroom,* http://www.demossnewspond.com/teen/presskit/TeenStats.htm.

7. Stephanie J. Ventura, et al., "Recent Trends in Teenage Pregnancy in the United States, 1990-2002," *CDC: National Center for Health Statistics,* http://www.cdc.gov/nchs/products/pubs/pubd/hestats/teenpreg1990-2002/teenpreg1990-2002.htm.

8. C. Everett Koop (as told to Dick Bohrer), "A Physician Speaks About Abortion," *Moody Monthly,* May 1980, http://www.pathlights.com/abortion/abort08.htm.

9. *Wikipedia,* s.v. "Abortion: By Personal and Social Factors," http://en.wikipedia.org/wiki/Abortion#By_personal_and_social_factors.

10. *Webster's II New College Dictionary,* s.v. "know."

11. Kerby Anderson, "Arguments Against Abortion," *Leadership U,* Updated August 5, 2003, http://www.leaderu.com/orgs/probe/docs/arg-abor.html.

12. Billy Graham Evangelistic Association, "Looking for Answers: Why is abortion such a big issue for Christians?," 2007, http://billygraham.org/LFA_Article.asp?ArticleID=29.

13. "Bald Eagle Protection Act," Summary from *Federal Wildlife Laws Handbook*, Chapter 4—State Summaries, http://ipl.unm.edu/cwl/fedbook/eagleact.html.

14. "House of Representatives Staff Analysis," *House Bill 399: Marine Turtles,* March 12, 2003, http://www.leg.state. fl.us/data/session/2003/House/bills/analysis/pdf/H0399c. nr.pdf.

15. David C. Reardon, "Psychological Reactions Reported After Abortion," *Eliot Institute*, 2006, http://www.abortionfacts. com/reardon/after_abortion_psychological_rea.asp.

16. Ibid.

Chapter 10

1. Jane Lampman, "Churches Confront an 'Elephant in the Pews,'" *The Christian Science Monitor,* August 25, 2005, http://www.csmonitor.com/2005/0825/p14s01-lire.html.

2. *Webster's II New College Dictionary,* s.v. "Trigger."

3. Bridget Maher, "Media Exposure Linked to Adolescent Sex," *Family Research Council,* http://www.frc.org/get. cfm?i=CU06D02.

4. Focus Adolescent Services, "Teen Sexual Behaviors: Issues and Concerns: The Range of Teenage Sexual Behavior," 1999, http://www.focusas.com/SexualBehavior.html.

Chapter 11

1. *Wikipedia,* s.v. "James Melville White," http://en.wikipedia.org/w/index.php?title=Mel_White.

2. "A Thorn in Their Side," *Southern Poverty Law Center: Intelligence Report,* Spring, 2005, http://www.splcenter.org/intel/intelreport/article.jsp?aid=525.

How to Accept Christ

If you're ready to accept Christ, why not pray this Bible-based prayer from your heart:

Lord God,

I repent of all of my sins and realize I'm a sinner who needs a Savior. This day I place trust in Jesus Christ, mankind's Savior, and the only way to heaven. I believe He died for my sins. I believe You raised Him from the dead!

Jesus, I call You Lord and God! Thank You for saving my soul! I commit today to follow You and live for You. Amen.

Speaking in Tongues

If you're a Christian who does not speak in other tongues but you're interested in learning more about it, please visit my Web site, www.pastorjoe.com. My three-lesson series titled "Pentecost Power" is available to view free of charge. In this series, you'll hear about how I received the gift of tongues, what the Bible has to say about this gift, and how you can receive it yourself. After you hear the series, if you're not convinced that the gift of tongues is for you, that's okay! It is always good to listen with an open mind, but God won't force anything on any of us. Remember, whether you speak in tongues or not, the Holy Spirit is in you!

About the Author

Joe Cameneti is the Senior Pastor of Believers' Christian Fellowship, located in his hometown, Warren, Ohio. Joe and his wife, Gina, pioneered BCF in 1983 after graduating from Bible school. In addition to pastoring a large church, Joe hosts a weekly teaching program called, "Pastor Joe," which airs on his Web site, www.pastorjoe.com as well as on television. God has gifted Pastor Joe with a unique teaching gift that makes the Bible practical, relevant, and easy to understand. Every time you hear him teach, you will walk away knowing how to implement the Word of God into your daily life, enabling you to grow spiritually and to know God better. Joe and Gina Cameneti are the parents of four children, Joseph Jr., David, Michele, and Deanna.

TO CONTACT THE AUTHOR

Joseph Cameneti Ministries
Believers' Christian Fellowship
P.O. Box 1949
Warren, OH 44482
1.877.330.3341
Web site: www.pastorjoe.com

Please include your testimony of help received from this book when you write. Your prayer requests are welcome.

*M*ost of us realize how important it is to use the Word of God when we pray. In his book, *"Extreme Prayer Makeover,"* Pastor Joe will teach you the *"REMODEL Prayer Card System"* that came to him supernaturally. Using this system you'll pray all 32 scriptures that the apostle Paul and others prayed, while covering 47 topics with ease! If you desire a consistent, confident prayer life that "avails much," then this book and prayer cards are a must!

Rescue from Evil
Expanded Love
More Boldness
Open Eyes
Deeper Desire
Extra Strength
Lord's Will

Book $13.99

Prayer Cards $8.00

Prayer Makeover Duo $19.95
(Includes book & prayer cards)

Prayer Makeover Bundle $29.95
(Includes book, 4 CD's, and prayer cards)

to order: 1.888.876.3118 (toll free) / www.shop.pastorjoe.com
For wholesale pricing call 1.877.330.3346 (toll free)

OTHER LIFE-CHANGING MESSAGES FROM PASTOR JOE